D1598546

A Handbook to
Sixteenth-Century Rhetoric

A Handbook to
Sixteenth-Century Rhetoric

Lee A. Sonnino

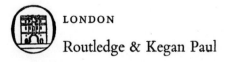
LONDON
Routledge & Kegan Paul

First published in 1968
by Routledge & Kegan Paul Limited
Broadway House 68-74 Carter Lane
London E.C.4.
Printed in Great Britain by
Alden & Mowbray Ltd at the Alden Press, Oxford

SBN 7100 2935 7

Contents

v

Preface

There has been until now no single work of reference to which the student of renaissance literature has been able to turn for information, even elementary, on all the aspects of the science of rhetoric for which (at even the most simple, literal level of inquiry) information is undoubtedly required. The various renaissance treatises in the vernacular all present their subject from one or another of several distinct points of view. It is not generally the case that the rhetoric of the author of one treatise is also the rhetoric which has been taught to a particular poet. The school texts, more widely known and therefore more probably known by a particular man, have been neither translated nor republished and are therefore rare. They are also difficult to read, being generally cryptic summaries of a subject learned by rote and written in difficult Latin (with the exception of Erasmus' *De copia*). In short, no one contemporary source contains all the information that is needed, nor provides it in a form suitable for reference.

I have attempted to gather together in this book the information provided by the various different authorities who contributed to the education of the renaissance author, particularly the writer in English.

These authorities include key classical rhetoricians he would probably
have read (at least in part), well-known and important renaissance
rhetoricians, and the writers of vernacular treatises and of major school
textbooks.

(I have arranged this information in a schematic and tabular form in
order that inquiry might start from the object, the particular rhetorical
form as it appears in a given literary text) The core of the book is the
central section on *elocutio*, the art of using the devices of rhetorical
ornament. In collating the descriptions of each figure available in
sixteenth-century and classical sources I have often had to select. My
principle of selection has been to include at least one 'standard' description, and all other descriptions which contain some feature of difference
or interest. The reason why more space has been given to *elocutio* in
this book is that *elocutio* is often the most fully treated topic in renaissance texts (although not necessarily in classical ones). Some popular
works such as Susenbrotus' *Epitome troporum ac schematum*, are concerned with *elocutio* alone, and *elocutio* was the part of rhetorical study
emphasised in schools. From the point of view of the needs of the
scholar now the aspect of rhetoric most clearly manifested in renaissance literature is the art of eloquent composition, the subtle craft of
deploying the schemes and tropes. One cannot begin to appreciate
this art until one knows what the schemes and tropes are. The philosophy of *inventio*, the methods of *pronunciatio* and *memoria*, although of
interest, are not so immediately necessary to the reader of renaissance
literature.

Although this book deals mainly with the methods and principles
of arranging, elaborating and presenting a rhetorical work of literature,
I have tried to include at least one definition of every rhetorical term
used in the sixteenth century. In this way basic information is provided
for *inventio*, *divisio* and so on, as well. I have provided, in a descriptive
index of the rhetorical figures at the close of the book, what I hope will
be an aid to finding the name of a particular figure when faced with an
example of it. This handbook is oriented towards the student of literature written in English, but may I believe be used with profit by those
studying the contemporary literatures of other languages.

I am indebted particularly to Dr. Alastair Fowler of Brasenose

College without whose encouragement this project would not have been started, and to Mr. Ewen Bowie of Corpus Christi College who has very kindly assisted me with the translations.

Oxford 1966

Introduction

Historical

The period we call the Renaissance is a subject of considerable historical
contention. What are its temporal boundaries? When did it begin?
When end? How is it to be distinguished from the period preceding it,
the Middle Ages? How may it be distinguished from the Baroque
that follows it (if we consider Mannerism to be a part of the late
Renaissance and not a separate epoch)? The subject of this book is the
rhetoric of the sixteenth century, particularly the rhetoric practised in
sixteenth-century England. I choose to consider that English literature
of this period lies within the Renaissance. As it shows many characteristics of the art we call Mannerist I must also add that I consider
Mannerist art belongs to the Renaissance rather than to the Baroque,
although it is of course a movement in the latter direction.

One can say for rhetoric that what distinguished this period from the
Middle Ages is not so much the knowledge of the existence of different
classical texts (although many were brought to light in the early
decades of the Italian Renaissance) as their availability, particularly
after the invention and spread of printing. It is this that distinguishes
the rhetoric taught and practised in England during the sixteenth century and the rhetoric of the preceding two centuries.

Medieval rhetoric placed before a student three kinds of text; accounts of rhetoric that formed part of a larger compendium of knowledge (for example that in the *De nuptiis Philologiae et Mercurii* of Martianus Capella or in the *Etymologiarum* of Isidore of Seville), some version of Cicero's *De inventione* or the pseudo-Ciceronian *Rhetorica ad Herennium* or some intelligent but more specialised work such as the *Ars versificatoria* of Matthew of Vendôme.

In sixteenth-century renaissance England the student of rhetoric had within his reach not only the printed work of Hermogenes, Cicero and Quintilian but also the treatises on rhetoric by lesser classical figures such as Aquila, Rutilius Lupus, Rufinianus, Sulpicius, Severianus and Consultus Chirius Fortunatianus. These were gathered into collections with such titles as *Antiqui rhetores* or *Rhetores latini et graeci*. The wealth of information available encouraged greater complexity in the works on rhetoric of learned contemporaries. (Learning in this branch of study seems to have been measured by quantity, not quality.) A book which stands at the apex of the tendency towards ridiculous detail is the almost unreadable *De universa ratione elocutionis rhetoricae* of Joannes Sturm, a monument to remorseless pedantry and tireless industry.

On the other hand the most important classical rhetoricians are also those whose works had the greatest influence on the pedagogic tradition of the sixteenth century. Renaissance rhetoric is based mainly upon the work of Cicero, Quintilian and the ubiquitous Auctor ad Herennium. The influence particularly noticeable in this period is that of Quintilian. Ben Jonson, educated towards the close of the century, remarked to Drummond that a thorough knowledge of Quintilian was all that a poet needed. Quintilian's schematic treatise on education (which includes a reworking of material from Cicero's more speculative discussions of the nature of oratory) forms the foundation for sixteenth-century rhetorical textbooks, of which the most intelligent is the *De copia verborum ac rerum* of Erasmus.

These texts are mentioned frequently in documents relating to English schools during the period;[1] Erasmus' *De copia*, the various *Tabulae de schematibus et tropis* of Mosellanus (Peter Schade), including

---

[1] See M. L. Clarke, *Classical Education in Britain* (Cambridge 1959), Ch. 1.

one table of the figures discussed by Erasmus in the *De copia*, and the *Epitome troporum ac schematum* of Susenbrotus. The most popular text appears to be that of Erasmus, which is not surprising as it is by far the best. It is elegant, sensible and intelligent, and well supplied with long examples which display the figures working together, a virtue completely absent from Mosellanus' enigmatic and typically fragmentary summaries. The arrangement of material in the *De copia* is unusual. Material often derived from Quintilian[1] is classified according to the way in which it assists the budding orator to amplify: by adding more words, by adding more impressive words, or by enlarging upon a subject with new, exciting and not entirely irrelevant thoughts, illustrations and examples. As most rhetorical devices add words or ideas to a passage, the bulk of those a student might need to know are found in the *De copia*. Erasmus displays a characteristically Renaissance affection for the visual and emblematic. For example, among the species of *exempla* he includes a section on the icon and on theological allegory, kinds of figuration not encouraged by the practical, forensic rhetoric of Quintilian.

At the beginning of the *Epitome* Susenbrotus cites these authorities; Cicero, Quintilian, Trapezuntius,[2] Erasmus, Melancthon, Diomedes Grammaticus, Donatus Grammaticus, Mancinellus, Martianus Capella, Fortunatianus and Veltkirchius.[3] He is indebted to most of these rhetoricians for examples only. Many of the definitions in the *Epitome* are taken directly from the *Ad Herennium*.[4] From Quintilian, or more probably from Quintilian via Melancthon, he takes his classification of the figures into tropes and schemes, and from Erasmus he takes (among other things) the treatment of the figures collected under the general concept of *hypotyposis* or vivid description. The *Epitome* itself discusses only the tropes and schemes, giving for each a description and one or two brief examples. Its importance lies in the fact that as a very popular

---

[1] Erasmus' methods for getting *copia* of thought relate closely to Quintilian's section on *amplificatio*, VIII, iv.

[2] George of Trebizond who taught in Rome at the turn of the fifteenth century.

[3] John Doelsch, the author of a very detailed commentary on Erasmus' *De copia*.

[4] For example, the definition of *commoratio* in the *Epitome*, p. 99 is identical to that in the *Ad Herennium*, IV, 53.

school textbook it inevitably came before many sixteenth-century writers at an early and impressionable age.

Another textbook used in schools was the *progymnasmata* or *prae-exercitamenes*. Two particular classical texts were used, Aphthonius and Hermogenes, the latter in Priscian's translation. This kind of text is a guide to composition, used in schools before pupils reached the stage of learning rhetoric and dialectic proper. It is made up of definitions, descriptions and examples of different genres of composition such as the fable, simple narrative, succinct statement, arguments against or in support of a proposition, composition by topic or headings, praise and vituperation, description and comparison. The most popular editions of these texts contained besides the original text copious notes, comments and extra examples supplied by a renaissance editor.[1]

The practice of adding textual notes (*scholia*) was also followed in the preparation of major classical texts for use in universities. By the end of the century the student was presented with a bewildering range of different editions and commentaries. In his *Ciceronianus* Gabriel Harvey distinguishes four schools of Ciceronian study; the school inspired by the dialectical and rhetorical teaching of the Greeks, those depending on Cicero and Quintilian alone, the Ramists, and the eclectics whose attention was given to obscurer features of thought and custom.[2]

Throughout the sixteenth century the study of rhetoric in English universities was based on the rhetorical works of Cicero. It was also suggested that the student read Quintilian, and derive a theoretical or philosophical understanding of the subject from Aristotle. Typical among the texts which would be recommended is the annotated version of Joannes Sturm, *Scholia ad rhetorica Aristotelis*. For the scholar Sturm provided editions of the works of Hermogenes: *De ratione inveniendi oratoria libri tres*, *De gravitate apta* in Sturm's translation and *De dicendi generis sive formis orationum libri duo*.

Nevertheless we have cause to doubt the apparent practice of this learning. In the *Rhetor* Harvey remarks:

---

[1] See for example the edition of Aphthonius by Reinhardt Lorich.
[2] See H. S. Wilson, 'Gabriel Harvey's Orations on Rhetoric', *ELH* 12 (1945), 167–82.

If they study this [Talaeus] they can dispense with their Mosellanus and Susenbrotus for Talaeus is far superior.[1]

Harvey is giving this advice to undergraduates, not to schoolchildren. It seems clear that despite the impressive range of annotated editions of classical authors most undergraduates learnt their rhetoric from the same texts they had been using at school. At best they would use books like Erasmus' *De copia* with a detailed and intelligent commentary by John Doelsch or Melancthon's *Elementorum rhetorices* explicated by Martin Crusius, and at the worst the dreary and unimaginative lists of definitions and examples of the above-mentioned Mosellanus and Susenbrotus.

These two lectures, the *Ciceronianus* and the *Rhetor*, published by Harvey in 1557, provide a guide to the development of rhetorical study under the influence of Peter Ramus, a time many believe to be crucial. Harvey recommends the use of the logic of Ramus[2] and the Ramistic rhetoric of Talaeus, instead of the traditional rhetorical schoolbooks and the commentaries on Cicero. In this way the student could avoid

> merely pointing out, as some have done, the ornaments of tropes and the embellishments of figures, without indicating the stores of arguments, the quantities of proofs, and the structural framework.[3]

If we can in fact see a shift of emphasis from ornament to structure in the *Rhetorica* of Talaeus then it would be correct to regard the text as fundamentally important. However, following Ramus' principle that *inventio* and *dispositio* are always properly parts of logic, Talaeus deals only with *elocutio* and *pronunciatio*, that is, only with ornament and delivery. Therefore as a text it teaches only that which Harvey wishes to avoid, the study of rhetorical ornament. Any change that there is in late renaissance rhetorical thinking stems from the dialectic text of Ramus which describes *inventio* and *dispositio* (content and structure) for any kind of verbal construct at all.

As a logic text Ramus' dialectic is a simplified version of traditional logic with rather 'arty' poetic examples taken mainly from Virgil. As a

---

[1] H. S. Wilson, p. 177.
[2] Peter Ramus, *Dialecticae libri duo* (Paris 1556).
[3] Gabriel Harvey, *Ciceronianus*, trans. C. A. Forbes (Lincoln, Nebraska 1945), p. 87.

rhetorical text, however, dealing with rhetorical invention and rhetorical disposition, it throws a great deal of weight on the logical structure of any written work and on the implicit correspondences between the material selected to illustrate an argument and the argument itself, and between the different parts of an argument as they are put together.

If we compare this rhetorically oriented dialectical treatment of *inventio* and *dispositio* with, for example, the rhetorical treatment of the same subject in *The Arte of Rhetorique* by Thomas Wilson, the nature of the change Ramus caused in more progressive teaching at the end of the sixteenth century becomes clear. Wilson simply lists the following *places* (categories or topics) about which material can be gathered (when discussing *things*): virtues, vices, towns, cities, castles, woods, waters, hills and mountains.[1] These topics are quite arbitrary and one does not naturally lead on to another. A discourse constructed only in this way must fail to be tightly knit.

For *inventio*, the process of amassing matter, Ramus provides an abstract system of connectives, spaces that the speaker may fill in and which, if correctly filled in, will form a coherent argument. For example, a subject may be discussed with respect to its causes and its effects. In such a discussion the speaker may choose to consider the effects, the essential cause or essence of his subject, the ways in which it differs from other things, how it was made—whether it was created or accumulated from saving and conserving, whether it occurred alone or with other things. Training in composition based on this kind of system for writing led eventually to poetry which gave a coherent definition of its subject instead of an arbitrarily selected list of qualities: for example,

> My love is of a birth as rare
> As 'tis for object strange and high:
> It was begotten by despair
> Upon Impossibility.[2]

[1] Thomas Wilson, *The Arte of Rhetorique* (1560), ed. G. H. Mair (Oxford 1909), p. 22.
[2] Andrew Marvell, 'The Definition of Love', *Poems* ed. H. Macdonald (London 1960), p. 34. In line 1 the subject is created spontaneously, in line 2 created alone, while lines 3-4 give its efficient cause.

It was the Ramistic synthesis of rhetoric with dialectic in the study and practice of amassing and arranging the content of any verbal structure which fired young teachers like Harvey and which led eventually to some modification in literary practice in the early part of the seventeenth century. Nevertheless one must point out that fine writers had produced coherent and cohesive verbal structures although their education had been quite independent of Ramistic concepts. Classical authorities such as Cicero and Quintilian have also emphasised the importance of coherence in the structure of an oratorical work.

> It is not enough merely to arrange the various parts: each several part has its own internal economy according to which one thought will come first, another second, another third, while we must struggle not merely to place these thoughts in their proper order but to link them together and give them such cohesion that there will be no trace of any suture: they must form a body, not a congeries of limbs.[1]

If we now consider the *Rhetorica* of Talaeus independently of the *Dialecticae* of Peter Ramus it becomes clear that alone it could have done nothing to encourage study of the content and structure of a text but would have provided only material for that consistently disintegrating attention to ornament alone which was the chief renaissance abuse of the classical tradition. Moreover the *Rhetorica* of Talaeus is unimaginative, derivative and badly written. It must be recognised for what it is, an unsightly appendage to the more elegant form with which Peter Ramus invested traditional logic.[2]

Renaissance rhetoric, as we have seen, differs from medieval rhetoric in the nature and numbers of the texts available. It is worth inquiring what distinguishes renaissance rhetoric from the classical Graeco-Roman rhetoric upon which it was based and whose texts were also readily accessible to the renaissance scholar. The difference does not lie in the texts (the texts were often the same): it lies in the purpose for which the texts were read and in the corresponding pedagogic idea of the complete practitioner of rhetorical art.

[1] Quintilian, *Institutio Oratoria*, trans. H. E. Butler (Loeb, Cambridge, Mass. 1953), VII, x, 16.

[2] See also W. J. Ong, *Ramus: method and the decay of dialogue* (Cambridge, Mass. 1958).

⌐The rhetoric of Cicero is based upon and directed towards a political orator, spokesman for and adviser to the rulers of a commonwealth. The Ciceronian orator is a man of public virtue, and eloquence is the torch by which he transmits his essential political understanding. For Quintilian, writing later under an empire, the good orator is a good man, a man of private virtue who exercises his eloquence for the individual. He is not a governor, he is a lawyer and the emphasis in the *Institutio* falls on forensic oratory whereas the *De Oratore* is also concerned with deliberative oratory, the discussion and decision of great collective causes.⌐

In the Renaissance we encounter a new phenomenon. The object of textbook attention is often a would-be writer, sometimes a poet. Several of the major original rhetorical works of the Renaissance are treatises on poetry which include a large section on rhetoric. The content of, for example, Scaliger's *Poetices* and the *Institutio* of Quintilian is in many places the same—many examples are drawn from the same source, the *Aeneid*—but the emphasis within the treatises is quite different. For Scaliger and for Puttenham and Minturno the orator whom their books are designed to assist is the poet.

The *Poetices libri septem* of Julius Caesar Scaliger is an important renaissance work on poetry, on all poetry. It aims to be universal. It discusses, for example, all the classical poetic genres known to late renaissance learning, whether they were much practised or not. Scaliger attempted to be at the same time historically descriptive and universally prescriptive. This plan is based of course on the humanistic axiom that the Greek and Latin classics encompass an imitable perfection and can provide rules and precedents for beauty. The *Poetices* opens with a discussion on the nature of poetry which for Scaliger is also the nature of the epic, the inclusive universal heroic poem in which we find examples of all the three styles (grand, medium and low) and which includes within its large scope examples of different, more limited genres. The *Poetices* contains large sections on style, on ornament, on the poetic metres and gives an historical and didactic account of the different classical genres of poetry.

Style, ornament, the nature of poetry and its history, its metres and rythms, are also subjects of two important vernacular treatises on poetry, Puttenham's *The Arte of English Poesie* and Minturno's *L'arte poetica*. Both these treatises have a section describing the poems that have been written in the genres practised, particularly in the vernacular. The interest of the vernacular treatise in this period is local and factual as opposed to the more ambitious attempt practised by the classical scholar to cover the whole subject.

The transubstantiation of the rhetorical text into a treatise on poetry is one result of the movement in the Renaissance away from the spoken word towards the word written or printed. The orator is no longer a speaker: he writes and, because little attention was paid in the sixteenth century to prose as literature, in these major treatises the orator is a poet. However, at another, more mundane level the prose writer is the object of rhetorical teaching. Among the most popular kinds of textbook in this period were books of instruction in the art of writing letters. Even the most noble brows of the century, those of Erasmus and Juan Luis Vives, bent to this task. As important political manœuvres were carried out by means of the letter, skill in its composition was vital to the sixteenth-century man of affairs.

While the sections in conventional textbooks devoted to delivery and the arts of memory in the sixteenth century withered and died, the handbooks of letter composition ran into several editions and sprouted appendices as new trees sprout leaves. Many of these texts were very intelligent. Addressed to the ambitious they could afford an urbane sophistication that is altogether lacking in the schoolbook. One of the most interesting of these texts is Sir John Hoskins' *Direccions for Speech and Style*. Here, in the introduction to a work devoted mainly to the composition of the letter we find a new place and a new significance for sentiments originally expressed by Cicero:

> The order of God's creatures in themselves is not only admirable and glorious, but eloquent: then he that could apprehend the consequence of things, in their truth, and utter his apprehensions as truly were a right orator.[1]

Eloquence is important to Hoskins because through eloquent persuasion important things are decided:

[1] Hoskins, *Direccions for Speech and Style*, ed. H. Hudson (Princeton 1935), p. 2.

The delivery of the most weighty and important things may be carried with such grace as it may yield pleasure to the conceit of the reader.[1]

Another feature of the rhetoric of the sixteenth century is the way in which it expresses the nationalistic movements towards the vernacular. Although ambitious linguistic patriotism is found more often in the more serious work such as those of Minturno and Puttenham than in the vernacular translations of school texts for the purposes of educating the vulgar, both kinds of treatise display a fundamental change of orientation away from the dead languages of learning to the language in which all kinds of things, business letters and epic verse, were actually being written. Rhetoric thus parallels the nationalistic and polemic sixteenth-century defence of poetry which is also a defence of the vernacular. *The Arte of English Poesie* is also a defence of the English language as a vehicle for poetry.

> And if the art of Poesy be but skill appertaining to utterance why may not the same be with us as well as with them, our language being no less copious pithy and significative than theirs, our conceits the same, and our wits no less apt to devise and imitate than theirs were? If again Art be but a certain order of rules prescribed by reason and gathered by experience, why should not Poesy be a vulgar Art with us as well as with the Greeks and Latins, our language admitting no fewer rules and nice diversities than theirs?[2]

In fact the full vernacular treatise on poetry (such as that of Puttenham) fuses into itself all the advanced tendencies of the time, the enthusiastic defence of the vernacular as a medium for poetry, the defence of the poetry written in the vernacular, the habit of thinking of the orator as a poet, and the inclusion in a treatise on poetry of the bulk of the information on composition provided by rhetoric.

Some theoretical implications of rhetorical practice

One of the important things bequeathed by Quintilian to the teaching of rhetoric was a systematic classification of the figures or colours into tropes and schemes. His differentiating principle is that some rhetorical

[1] Hoskins, p. 7.
[2] George Puttenham. *The Arte of English Poesie*, ed. G. D. Willcock and A. Walker (Cambridge 1936), p. 5.

figures vary a passage by altering a word from its ordinary meaning to another, abnormal meaning whereas other figures do not. The fundamental trope is metaphor, whereby a word is transferred from its place in the code of language to another place or meaning when there is no word available or where the metaphor is more expressive in the particular context than the usual word. Other tropes makes this transference: metonymy and *synecdoche* (species of metaphor), *pronominatio* and *onomatopoeia*.

However allegory, irony, circumlocution, *hyperbaton* and hyperbole are also tropes. We can perceive the metaphoric nature of allegory, irony and even hyperbole in which the exaggerated terms do not have their ordinary meaning but signify something less. Wherein lies the change of meaning in circumlocution? The feature circumlocution has in common with metaphor is that it substitutes one or more words for another, expected word. Similarly, in *hyperbaton* the words displaced substitute one for another, in this case by place. Although it is not Quintilian's definition, a sufficient characteristic of a trope is the capacity of substituting one or more words for other words.

A definition of the trope based upon the capacity to substitute can be much more inclusive. Scaliger has made a classification of the figures in which most are classed as tropes. He conceives the trope as the figure which substitutes either words for words or the fictive for the real, thus including figures of pretence like *rogatio*, the pretended question, and *confessio*, the false admission. These figures all involve some alteration in the position and the meaning of words. They are of five general kinds; those which describe vividly (under *tractatio*), those which exaggerate (under *hyperbole*), those which diminish or omit (under *eclipsis*), allegory and irony. This system implies that no literary process can occur without continually using tropes, and conversely that the process of transmuting reality into art is also the process which creates the trope.

Of the schemes and tropes Quintilian admits that

> the resemblance between the two is so close that it is not easy to distinguish between them . . . for example while irony belongs to schemes of thought just as much to tropes, *periphrasis*, *hyperbaton* and *onomatopoeia* have been ranked by distinguished authors as schemes of words rather than tropes.[1]

[1] Quintilian, IX, i, 3.

11

the style's the content

He defines a scheme as that which 'does not necessarily involve any alternation of the order or the strict sense of the words'.[1] Nevertheless it can be argued that even simple repetition causes a change of meaning:

> The schemes are divided into two groups, schemes of thought (*dianoias*), that is of the mind, feeling or conceptions . . . and schemes of words (*lexeos*) that is of diction, expression, language or style.[2]

This whole apparatus is clumsy and confusing. It seems to me that any variation of the configuration of words inevitably affects what the words express. Worse, the Latin phrases *figura sententiarum* and *figura verborum* have led to a useless division being made in such rhetorics as the *soi disant* 'logical' rhetoric of Audomarus Talaeus, between figures which alter phrases or passages and those which affect only single words. Probably there is no consistent organic classification possible for material derived originally from the diverse practices of individuals and of schools. Rhetoric did not begin as a science, it began as an art, at its best an art of expression, at its worst an art of deception.

Finally in this introduction I should like to comment on the renaissance treatment of two figures which have assumed tremendous importance in contemporary criticism: irony and ambiguity. Technically renaissance *ironia* is a much more limited concept than the rather too catholic one we understand by the word 'irony'. *Ironia* is that figure in which a word or phrase or whole passage means the contrary of what it appears to mean. The species of *ironia* include sarcasm and the urbane joke. In one way or another they all involve an implication of the opposite meaning. This concept is more limited than present usage, for which an ironic statement is one that, while stating one thing, implies the existence of something different. The Renaissance did have a term for this second phenomenon: *emphasis*, the property of a statement which has implications or levels of meaning beyond the merely literal. *Ironia* itself, although confined to contraries, could be present throughout extended sequences of words, whole passages or works.

For example, in Shakespeare's *Macbeth*, *ironia* is initiated by the prophecies of the witches, which appear to be false but are learnt to be

---

[1] *ibid.* IX, i, 7.
[2] *ibid.* IX, i, 17.

true. At the end of the play Macbeth discovers that from the point of view of the value rather than the fact of kingship the witches' prophecies were not true at all. The *ironia* of this play causes an uncertainty about whether any statement made in the play is true or false, that is, whether it means what it says or the contrary of what it says. It is not our broader irony, which creates uncertainty about the nature of a thing but not about whether it exists.

Quintilian, training lawyers, disliked and distrusted ambiguity, the property of meaning two or more things at once. More original renaissance writers such as Puttenham admit that ambiguity can have a purpose.[1] The *Rhetorica ad Herennium* also states that ambiguity can be a means of emphasising some point when a statement means two things but only one is understood.

When we look at renaissance literary practice, particularly towards the end of the period, we find that ambiguous statement is often present, both in the form that obtains emphasis from the suppression of one side of a double meaning, and in the form that, assisted by the context, supports both meanings. Painting at the end of the Renaissance, in the style we call Mannerist, also displays ambiguity. In a deposition by Pontormo the figures are neither angels nor men but both.

The sonnets of Shakespeare, a late work in a strong renaissance form, are in themselves a tissue of ambiguities. The ultimate meaning of the Shakesperian sonnet appears to depend on the resolved composite meanings of all the ambiguities present in the poem. For example the meaning of the line

Suns of the world may stain when heaven's sun staineth[2]

depends not only on the resultant meaning of the repeated *sun/son* pun and the pun on *stain* and *staineth* but also on the uncertainty built up in the poem between contraries such as *golden* in line 4 and *gilded* in line 5.

In renaissance rhetorical theory ambiguity is barely touched upon, yet in later renaissance poetic practice it is exploited to the full. Our present attention to the possibilities of ambiguous statement and the intensification of significance and feeling obtained by the simultaneous

[1] Puttenham, p. 261.
[2] William Shakespeare, *Works*, ed. Peter Alexander (London 1951), p. 1313.

13

recognition of more than one possible meaning is therefore justified. Although in this handbook I am concerned with historical material only, it would be foolish to maintain that this is all that one needs in order to read sixteenth-century poetry with full understanding. On the other hand it is even greater folly to believe that one can do without a knowledge of the things that these writers knew, particularly the things they had impressed upon them repeatedly in their years at school.

The Figures or Colours of Rhetoric: Latin Names

Abominatio (Bdelygmia)
also known as *fastidium*

Erasmus (37)
For plenitude of words. A means of colouring one's style. Another figure may be changed by the use of this.

Peacham (82)
Signifies how much a speaker hateth and abhorreth some person, word, deed etc. . . . commonly in a short form and in few words . . . not to be used either against things worthy of love or things indifferent.

EXAMPLES

Peacham (82)
Against a person thus: Out upon him wretch.
Against an odious word thus: Peace for shame.
Against an odious deed, thus: Fie upon it.

THE FIGURES OR COLOURS OF RHETORIC: LATIN NAMES

Against an odious thing, thus: Away with it, I love not to hear of it, I abhor it: Avoid Satan.

Sometime with more words, thus: No more for shame, bury it in silence, whose eyes can look upon it, and not loath it, or whose ears can hear it, and not abhor it?

Abusio (Catachresis)
also known as *audacia*

Ad Herennium (IV, 45)
The inexact use of a like and kindred word in place of the precise and proper one.

Quintilian (VIII, vi, 34f)
Trope. By this term is meant the practice of adapting the nearest available term to describe something for which no actual term exists ... *abusio* is employed where there is no proper term available, *metaphor* when there is another term available.

Susenbrotus (10)
Trope. The practice of adapting the nearest available term to describe something for which no proper term exists. . . . Therefore it differs from a metaphor which changes the proper term into another one.

Hoskins (11)
More desperate than a metaphor. It is the expressing of one matter by the name of another which is incompatible with it, and sometimes clean contrary.

EXAMPLES

Wilson (174f)
As in calling some water, a fish pond, though there be no fish in it at all: or else when we say, here is long talk, and small matter. Which are spoken unproperly, for we cannot measure, either talk or matter, by length, or breadth.

16

Puttenham (180)

I *lent my love to loss* . . . lent is properly of money or some such thing
. . . and being applied to love is utterly abused.

Hoskins (11)

I gave order to some servants of mine, whom I thought as apt for such
charities as myself, to lead him out into the forest and there to kill him,
(where *charity* is used for *cruelty*). The abuse of a word drawn from
things far different, as, Being sister in nature, I wish I were not so far off
akin in fortune. By fine conversants of our time, when they strain for
an extraordinary phrase, as, He threatens me a good turn.

Cicero
Erasmus, Melancthon, Susenbrotus, Talaeus, Day, Peacham[1]

Acclamatio (Epiphonema)

Quintilian (VIII, v, 11)

Under *sententia*. An exclamation attached to the close of a statement
or proof by way of climax.

Erasmus (82)

For plenitude of thought. A climax in the form of an exclamation at
the end of a narrative or proof . . . epigrams end with this.

Susenbrotus (96)

Scheme. The summing up of things narrated or proposed. If these can
be put together well this device has much acuteness. It is especially
suited to the epigram and epilogue in which the most important points
of the argument are condensed and drummed into the minds of the
hearers. . . . Useful for *dehortatio* and *adhortatio* [see also ADHORTATIO].

Scaliger (III, xl)

Under *tractatio*. After dealing with a thing or a deed, a *sententia* is added
expressing admiration or disapproval. . . . This may be done by the
persona of the poet.

[1] These names following the discussion of certain figures are the names of other
classical (first line if there are any) and renaissance (following line) authors in
whose works (listed under *The texts used in compiling this work*, p. 240) a mention
or description of the figure may be found.

Hoskins (34f)
A sententious clause of a discourse or report such as Daniel in his poems concludes with perpetually ... serves for amplification when after a great crime or desert ... it gives a moral note worth ... observation ... It sometimes expresses the cause and reason of a former *narratio*.

EXAMPLES

Fraunce (76)
When he had manifested the inconstancy of the people, and settled perseverance of *Philanax* and *Euarclius*, he addeth:
So evil balanced be the extremities of popular minds, and so much natural imperiousness there rests in a well framed spirit.

Puttenham (217)
>   What medicine then, can such disease remove
>   Where love breeds hate, and hate engenders love.

Hoskins (34f)
After the true relation of Scipio Africanus his course ... it may be folded up in this acclamation:
So little need hath he to stoop to private cases that thrives upon public victories, and so small leisure hath he to be desirous of riches, being but the means, who hath been so long possessed of honour, which is the mortal end of mortal actions.

Rufinianus
Erasmus, Melancthon, Day, Peacham

Accusatio (Categoria)
also known as *criminis reprehensio*

Peacham (80f)
Scheme. Openeth and detecteth some secret wickedness of his adversary, and layeth it open before his face ... must not be false ... requireth a serious and sharp form.

18

EXAMPLES

Peacham (80f)

He that dippeth his hand with me in the dish, he shall betray me.

O full of all subtlety and all mischief, thou child of the devil, and enemy of all righteousness, wilt thou not cease to pervert the straight ways of the Lord?

Cicero

Acervatio (Polysyndeton)

Quintilian (IX, iii, 50ff)

Scheme. The opposite of ... *asyndeton* ... characterised by the number of connecting particles employed ... we may repeat the same ... particle or they may be different ... Adverbs and pronouns may also be varied ... these figures make our utterances more vigorous and emphatic.

Susenbrotus (37f)

Partly scheme and partly trope. The use of many different conjunctions. ... It is a figure of the higher poetic style (*magis*) rather than the familiar style of speech (*familiaris*).

Scaliger (III, xliii)

Under *tractatio*. A prescribed accumulation, although not always in a particular order ... for an easier and lower style of argument.

Peacham (53)

A figure which knitteth the parts of an oration with many conjunctions ... to knit many things together of like nature ... and to separate contrary matters asunder ... may be called the chain of speech forasmuch as every chain has conjunction of matter, and a disjunction of links.

EXAMPLES

Puttenham (175)

And I saw it, and I say it and I will swear it to be true.

Peacham (53)
For I am sure that neither death, neither life, neither angels, neither rule, neither power, neither things present, neither things to come, neither height, neither depth, neither any other creature shall be able to separate us from the love of God.

Rutilius Lupus
Erasmus, Melancthon, Day

Adhortatio (Protrope)

Scaliger (III, cv)
Itself a kind of figure, it comes under the general heading of *deliberatio* or argument. It covers *sapientia* (*paraeneticos*), *admonitio* (*nutheticos*), *consolatio* (*paramythia*) and includes *dehortatio*, which is to promote the opposite.

Peacham (77f)
Form of speech by which the orator exhorteth and persuadeth his hearers to do something . . . not only the form of a commandment or of a promise . . . but also gives reasons.

EXAMPLES

Peacham (78)
If ever God have had respect to a just cause, or ever gave victory where it was due, or ever lent his hand to equity against tyranny, or ever preferred his people, and confounded his enemies, he will this day fight with us, and for us, and give us a glorious victory, be our enemies never so many, and we never so few, and therefore shew yourselves this day valiant, courageous and constant, fight this day for your honour, and for your country, cast off this day all fear that may make you weak and arm yourselves with hope that may make you strong.

Adinventio (Pareuresis)

Peacham (95f)
Scheme. The speaker alleges a premeditated excuse containing reasons

of such might as are able to vanquish all objections ... and repel all violence and force of ... accusations, ... requests or ... complaints.

EXAMPLE
Peacham (95f)
Aeneas in the 4th book of the *Aeneid* ... First, she objecteth by her suspicion ... his unkind and and wicked purpose to steal away from here ... Secondly, she telleth him that for his sake, she is hated of foreign princes and despised of her own people. ... Aeneas maketh an answer confuting of many parts as followeth: First he confesseth her kindness, goodness and liberality. Secondly, he denieth that ever his intent was to depart by stealth. Thirdly he telleth her that wedlock was never his meaning ... fourthly ... he greatly desireth to restore Troy ... Fifthly, the oracle of Apollo calleth him from Carthage to Italy. ...

Ad Herennium

Adjudicatio (Epicrisis)
one kind of *acclamatio* (see under ACCLAMATIO)

Peacham (99)
Scheme. When reciting a sentence or saying of some author, the orator adds and delivers his opinion or judgment upon it ... praise or dispraise, or in giving light to it, which is best performed in a short addition.

EXAMPLE
Peacham (99)
An example of our Saviour Christ, saying: Ye have heard that it was said to them of old time, Thou shalt not commit adultery, but I say unto you, that whosoever looketh on a woman to lust after her, hath committed adultery with her already in his heart.

Trapezuntius

Adjunctio (Zeugma)

also known as *epizeugmenon* and *junctio* (with parts *prejunctio, media 'unctio* and *postjunctio*)

Cicero (De Oratore III, liv, 206)
Scheme. One verb may be made to serve the purpose of a number of clauses.

Quintilian (IX, iii, 62)
Scheme. In which a number of clauses are all completed by the same verb, which would be required by each singly if they stood alone.

Puttenham (163f)
Scheme. More clauses than one ... some such word be supplied to perfect the congruity or sense of them all ... *Prozeugma*: supply at the forefront of several clauses ... *Mezozeugma*: in the middle of the clauses he serves ... *Hypozeugma*: not before nor in the middle, ... after the clauses.

EXAMPLES

Peacham (51)
For neither art thou the *Catiline*, whom at any time shame could call back from dishonesty, either fear from peril or reason from madness.
The people of Rome destroyed *Numance*, then *Carthage*, cast down *Corinth*, overthrew *Frigellas*.

Hypozeugma ... the foundation of freedom, the fountain of equity, the safeguard of wealth, and custody of life, is preserved by laws.

Ad Herennium, Rufinianus
Erasmus, Melancthon, Susenbrotus, Sherry, Scaliger, Day

Admiratio (Thaumasmos)

Erasmus (37)
For plenitude of words. The colouring of an expression may be changed through the use of *admiratio*, which may also lead to a change of figure.

22

Peacham (72f)
Scheme. The orator declareth how much he marvelleth at some thing
... emphatical, ... in praising, ... in dispraising.

EXAMPLES

Peacham (72)
He doth great things and unsearchable, yea marvellous things without
number.
O the deepness of the riches, of the wisdom and knowledge of God.

Cicero

Admonitio (Paraenesis)

also known as *nutheticos, sapientia*

Scaliger (III, cv)
Under *deliberatio, adhortatio, paraenesis*: the precepts that may be
understood from wise sayings. [That is, both *paraenesis* and *nutheticos*
urge some action through warning or precept—see under ADHOR-
TATIO.]

Peacham (78f)
Scheme. Warning. Properly to reveal dangers and dehort the reader
from them.

EXAMPLES

Peacham (78f)
For God's sake take heed Judges lest through hope of present peace you
bring not in continual war.
Beware of false prophets which come unto you in sheep's clothing, but
inwardly they are ravening wolves, you shall know them by their fruits.

Quintilian

Adnarratio

Scaliger (III, lxxiii)
Under *tractatio*. This figure is a narrative introduced into our oration
covering what our opponent may say against us in order to distort or

C   23

obscure his case. The material this narrative contains need not always be contrary to our argument: we may use it to assist our own case.

EXAMPLE
Scaliger (III, lxxiii)
In Book X of the *Aeneid* Juno, using this figure, inserts into her own speech a speech supposedly spoken by Venus, before Venus herself speaks.

Adnominatio (Polyptoton)
also known as *paregmenon, paronomasia* (Quintilian) or under the generic heading *traductio* (Auctor ad Herennium)

Cicero (*Orator*, XXXIX, 135)
We may . . . introduce the same word repeatedly in different cases.

Quintilian (IX, iii, 66f)
Scheme. *Paronomasia.* . . . This may be effected in different ways. It may depend on the resemblance of one word to another which has preceded, although the words are in different cases.

Quintilian (IX, iii, 37)
Polyptoton. The repetition of a stem word with a variation of cases [later the word *paronomasia* used for another figure. See under ALLUSIO.]

Susenbrotus (52)
Scheme. The same word is repeated a number of times in different cases. . . . This not only does not strike harshly on the ears but in this way makes the prose sound even more harmonious.

Peacham (55)
Scheme. A figure which of the word going before deriveth the word following. . . . To delight the ear by the derived sound and to move the mind with a consideration of the high affinity and concord of the matter.

EXAMPLES
Fraunce (52)
> Thou art of blood, joy not to make things bleed:
> Thou fearest death, think they are loth to die.

24

Peacham (55)
The wisdom of the wise.

Hoskins (17)
> Exceedingly exceeding that exceedingness,
> By this faulty using of our faults.

(The same word in several cases) For fear hid his fear.
(The same verb in several voices) Forsaken by all friends and forsaking all comfort.
(The same adjective in several comparisons) Much may be said in my defence, much more for love, and most of all for that divine creature which hath joined me and love together.

Rutilius Lupus, Aquila, Rufinianus
Trapezuntius, Melancthon, Susenbrotus, Talaeus, Day

Aequipollentia (Isodunamia)

Erasmus (33f)
For plenitude of words. An excellent method of varying. It consists in the addition, taking away or doubling of a negative and in opposing words . . . effects at once a new form of speech . . . may be predicated only of those things which are capable of opposites.

EXAMPLE

Erasmus (33f)
He is not among the last (instead of *he was not first*).

Alliteratio (Parimion)

also known as *paronomasia* (not to be confused with *allusio*)

Puttenham (174)
Melodious . . . every word of the verse to begin with a like letter.

Peacham (49f)
Scheme. A kind of repetition. Beginneth diverse words with one and the same letter making the sentence more ready for the tongue and

more pleasant to the ear ... pleasure in repetition joined with variety.
... Found particularly in poetry, in a proverb or short sentence.

EXAMPLES

Peacham (50)
When friendly favour flourished I found felicity but now no hope doth
help my heart in heaviness so hard.
To hold with the hare, and hunt with the hound.

Hoskins (15f)
Rhymes running in rattling rows.

Hector, Hanno, Hannibal dead, Pompey, Pyrrhus spilled;
Cyrus, Scipio, Caesar slain, and Alexander killed.
(Both examples of excess.)

Rutilius Lupus

Allusio (Paronomasia or **Prosonomasia)**
also known as *agnominatio, adnominatio, paulum immutatum verbum* (not
to be confused with *adnominatio* or *alliteratio*)

Cicero (*De Oratore*, III, liv, 206)
Slight changes and alterations may be made in words.

Wilson (201)
Scheme. When we take a letter, or a syllable from some word, or else
add a letter, or syllable to a word.

Scaliger (IV, xxxiii)
Scheme. Words which are similar in sound but which through slight
alteration differ in meaning. Not to be used in serious poetry. Appropriate for epigrams, satires, comedy, at its most graceful when from
one word by a slight alteration we extract the contrary.

Peacham (56)
Scheme. A figure which declineth into a contrary by a likelihood of
letters either added, changed or taken away. ... Commonly used to
illude ... light and illuding form.

EXAMPLES

Wilson (142)

And please your grace you have so many frauditours, so many conveyors and so many deceivers...He should have said auditors, surveyors and receivers.

Puttenham (202f)

Tiberius...Biberius.

> And all my life I will confess
> The less I love, I live the less.

Hoskins (16)

Alas, what can saying make them believe whom seeing cannot persuade?

And whilst he was followed by the valiantest, he made a way for the vilest.

...our fasting into feasting.

Ad Herennium, Rutilius Lupus, Rufinianus
Trapezuntius, Susenbrotus, Talaeus, Fraunce, Puttenham, Day

Ambiguitas (Amphibologia)

Ad Herennium (IV, 67)

A mean of emphasis. When one word can be understood in two or more senses but is understood in the sense the speaker intends.

Vice. When it causes the speech to be obscure, and thus confuses its meaning. It will be easy to find ambiguities, if we know and pay heed to the multiple meanings of words.

Cicero (*De Oratore*, II, lxi, 250)

Bon-mots prompted by ambiguity are deemed the very wittiest, though not always concerned with jesting, but often even with what is important.

Quintilian (VII, ix)

[This whole chapter is devoted to ambiguity in oratory. It is not treated as a figure, ornament or vice. Quintilian warns against the dangers of ambiguity in legal matters. It is to be avoided or, if unavoidable, resolved.]

27

Quintilian (IX, ii, 70)
Vice. It is important too that a figure should not depend on ambiguous collocations of words (a trick which is far more foolish than the last).

Puttenham (260f)
Vice. When we speak or write doubtfully and that the sense may be taken two ways ... to be avoided unless [the orator] does it for the nonce and to some purpose.

EXAMPLES

Peacham (1577, G^v)
I suppose you said *Myrrina* told you that *Bacchis* hath her ring. (We do not know whose ring, Bacchis' or Myrrina's.)
I will show you the city standing on a high hill, twenty miles before you come to it. (The city or the observer stands on a hill?)
His mistress would give her a mark besides her wage before the year went about. (Is it a mark of money or a mark on the head or shoulders?)

Fortunatianus
Sherry, Wilson, Scaliger

Amplificatio

Quintilian (VIII, iii, 90)
The way in which style may elevate or depress the subject in hand ... the first means of stylistic ornament, amplification or attenuation ... (a) in the actual word employed to describe a thing ... (b) by the four principle methods of *amplification*: *incrementum, comparatio, ratiocinatio* and *congeries*.

Wilson (116f)
Scheme. If either we purpose to make our tale appear vehement, to seem pleasant, or to be well stored with much copy ... in praising or dispraising ... by means of *sententia*, proverbs ... things notable in this life ... consisteth most in augmenting and diminishing of any matter.

Peacham (120f)
Class of schemes. Of words . . . a very great word put for another not so great . . . or when a less word is put for a word not so little. . . .
Of things, when things themselves are repeated and amplified. . . . It increases matters or enriches the oration with apt and pleasant speech.

EXAMPLES
Wilson (121)
When I see one sore beaten, to say he is slain: to call a naughty fellow, thief or hangman, when he is not known to be any such.
It is an offence to bind a citizen of Rome with chains, it is an heinous deed to whip him: it is worse than manslaughter to kill him: what shall I call it to hang him up upon a gibbet?

Wilson (123)
My servants in good sooth, if they feared me in such sort, as all the citizens do fear thee: I would think it best for me to forsake my house.

Peacham (122)
Examples . . . are plentiful and almost everywhere to be found in the orations of *Tully*. He doth amplify the thefts, the sacrileges, the robberies, the lecherous life of *Verres*, and also his new devised pains and punishments: the drunkenness, the bold presumptions, the prodigality . . . of *Antony* . . . and most vehemently of all against *Catiline*.

Ad Herennium, Cicero, Rufinianus, Fortunatianus
Trapezuntius, Erasmus, Melancthon, Susenbrotus, Sherry, Scaliger, Puttenham, Hoskins

Ante occupatio (Procatalepsis)
also known as *praeoccupatio, praeventio*

Cicero (*Orator*, xl, 138)
To anticipate the objections to one's argument that might be perceived by one's opponent.

Wilson (188)
Scheme. When we prevent those words that another would say and disprove them . . . or . . . answer unto them . . . Sometimes this figure is used when we say we will not speak this or that and yet do notwithstanding.

Fraunce (100)
Scheme. When we prevent and meet with that which might be objected and do also make answer to the same . . . first part *preoccupatio* or the laying down of the objection . . . the second subjection, or answering thereto so that commonly there is a kind of *prosopopoeia* adjoined unto it.

EXAMPLES
Wilson (188)
I hear one say, Sir . . . what were we the worse, if we had no scripture at all? To whom he answered: the Scripture is left unto us by God's own will.
Such a one is an officer, I will not say a briber.

Fraunce (101)
An unused thing it is . . . that a woman should give public counsel to men. . . . For certainly a woman may well speak to such men who have forgotten all manlike government.

Peacham (183)
Thou wilt say then unto me, why then blameth he us yet? For who hath been able to resist his will? But O man who art thou which disputeth with God? Shall the pot say to the potter, why madest thou me in this fashion?

Rufinianus
Melancthon, Scaliger, Puttenham, Day

Appositum (Epitheton)
also known as *sequens, attributum*

Quintilian (VIII, vi, 40f)
Trope. This figure gives to a word an appropriate adjective . . . to

adorn and enhance the style. . . . Poets employ it with special frequency and freedom . . . but in oratory an epithet is redundant unless it . . . adds something to the meaning. . . . Its decorative effect is greatest when it is metaphorical. . . . If separated from the word to which it belongs it has a significance of its own and becomes an *antonomasia* [see under PRONOMINATIO].

Susenbrotus (39)
Scheme. It is used for the purposes of ornament, for vituperation or for evaluating the subject being discussed.

Scaliger (III, xxvii)
Scheme. It combines with *hyperbole, metaphor,* and other figures . . . and may express admiration, indignation or contempt.

EXAMPLES
Puttenham (176)
Diana the chaste and thou lovely Venus.

Peacham (147)
We pray for all princes, that their life may be long, their kingdoms secure, their court safe, their armies strong, their counsellors trusty, their people good.
The judgments of almighty God are great, just, unsearchable, marvellous and mighty.
O happy Prince of such worthy Counsellors: O happy Counsellors of so worthy a Prince.

Erasmus, Susenbrotus, Sherry, Puttenham, Day

Articulus (Brachylogia)
(not to be confused with *incisum* or *dissolutio*)

Ad Herennium (IV, 26)
Scheme. When the intervals between single words in staccato speech are distinguished by pauses or commas.

Susenbrotus (53)
Scheme. When we have single words, the intervals between which are distinguished by pauses indicated by commas.

Puttenham (213)
Scheme. To proceed all by single words, without any close or coupling, saving that a little pause or comma is given to every word ... (distinguished from *asyndeton* which places a comma between clauses.)

Peacham (57)
Scheme. Setteth one word from another by cutting the oration ... with commas ... for brevity, ... convenient to express any vehement affections.

EXAMPLES

Puttenham (213)
Envy, malice, flattery, disdain.

Peacham (57)
Thou hast lost thy substance, thy good name, thy friends, thy parents.
I will make them to be a reproof, a proverb, a scorn, a shame, I will make them desolate, waste, despised, hissed at and accursed.

Rutilius Lupus
Veltkirchius, Sherry, Day

Asseveratio
also known as *obtestatio* (but not to be confused with *obsecratio* known as *obtestatio*)

Scaliger (III, xxxviii)
Under *tractatio*. Adds to the force of the original poposition. We choose the most appropriate and forceful oaths according to the skill, sex, state or age of the subject.

EXAMPLES

Scaliger (III, xxxviii)
For a strong man: by your right hand.
For Dido: by those tears.

Attemperatio

Scaliger (III, xxxvi)
Under *tractatio*. A method by which we firmly establish the truth of
what we are about to say ... by adding, for example, *sententiae* introduced by a character, or from a poet, or in parentheses.

EXAMPLE

Scaliger (III, xxxvi)
I believe therefore (and this is no empty faith). ...

Attributio

Scaliger (III, xlviii)
Under *tractatio*. When to things or persons we attribute things or
persons, manners, speeches and so on. ... We may attribute qualities
of a person to a person, qualities of a thing to a person, qualities of a
person to a thing. ... Our attributions may be direct or indirect ...
attributio also covers *prosopopoeia* which is a special class of attributions.

EXAMPLES

Scaliger (III, xlviii)
Tempestuous weather, silent nights.
The temple of Dido's most beautiful form.

Aversio (Apostrophe)

Quintilian (IX, ii, 38f)
Scheme. It consists in the diversion of our address from the judge
[to some other] ... our adversary ... or some invocation to a god, mute

object, country etc. . . . The term *apostrophe* is also applied to utterances that divert the attention of the hearer from the question before them.

Peacham (116f)
Scheme. The orator turneth suddenly from the former frame of his speech to another . . . a sudden removing from the third person to the second.

Hoskins (48)
A turning of your speech to some new person . . . sometimes . . . to some quality, or thing, that yourself gives show of life to.

EXAMPLES

Fraunce (82)
   Pan, father Pan, the god of silly sheep.

Fraunce (83)
   . . . O muse historify
   Her praise, whose praise to learn your skill hath framed me.

Fraunce (84)
   Alas poor lute, how much thou art deceived . . .

Peacham (116)
O Israel thine iniquity hath undone thee.

Hoskins (48)
And herein you witnesses are to consult with your own consciences, . . .
Did you mark his looks?
Hope, tell me, what hast thou to hope for?

Aquila, Rufinianus
Melancthon, Susenbrotus, Talaeus, Puttenham, Day

Benedictio (Eulogia)

Scaliger (III, cx)
Under praise. When we utter for any subject the most apt and obvious predicates . . . those which are simple, brief and true. . . . Used in the low style.

Peacham (65)
Scheme. By which the orator pronounceth a blessing upon some person for the goodness that is in him or her ... doth much move to the love of the thing which is the cause of blessedness.

EXAMPLES

Peacham (65)
Blessed are ye of the Lord, that ye have shewed such kindness unto your Lord *Saul*, that you have buried him.
Blessed are those servants, whom the Lord when he cometh shall find waking.

Benevolentia (Philophronesis)
also known as *exceptio benigna*

Robertellus (49)
This figure is used for flattering an enraged opponent, from Demetrius Phalaerus.

Peacham (96f)
Scheme. The speaker, perceiving the might of his adversary to be too great against him useth gentle speech, fair promises and humble submission to mitigate the rigour and cruelty of his adversary ... to move compassion ... and obtain grace and mercy.

EXAMPLES

Peacham (96f)
Jacob to *Esau* ... calling him his lord, and himself his servant.
Behold we are the servants of *Nabucodonozor* the great king, we lie down before thee, use us as shall be good in thy light, behold our houses and all our places ... and all our lodges and tabernacles lie before thy face: use them as it pleaseth thee.

Ad Herennium

35

Boni ominis captatio (Euphemismos)

Peacham (89f)
Scheme. A prognostication of good . . . by which the orator inter-preteth an uncertain thing to the better part, or else declareth before that some good thing shall come to pass afterward.

EXAMPLES
Peacham (89f)
I exhort you to be of good courage, for there shall be no loss of any mans life among you, but of the ship only.
Of some good man now dead . . . I speak of him that is in heaven.

Quintilian

Castigatio

Scaliger (III, lxxxii)
Under *eclipsis*. It is not a process of verbal depreciation, but depreciates by introducing base ideas, examples and comparisons. We may respond in the same way with better arguments, or to the contrary.

EXAMPLES
Scaliger (III, lxxxii)
I did not swear with the Greeks at Aulis to annihilate the Trojan people.

Certitudo (Asphalia)
also known as *securitas*

Peacham (68f)
Scheme. By which the speaker persuadeth a security and safety to his hearer by offering himself as a surety for the confirmation of his warrant.

EXAMPLES
Peacham (68)
Juda persuading . . . *Jacob* to let *Benjamin* . . . go into *Aegypt* with the rest of his brothers . . . I will be surety for him, of my hand shalt thou

require him, if I bring him not to thee, then let me hear the blame for ever.

In a mighty form: My blood for thy blood, my life for thy life, my soul for thy soul.

Circumductio (Perissologia)

also known as *macrologia, supervacuo*

Quintilian (VIII, vi, 61)
Vice. Where *circumlocutio* passes into excess ... which is a positive hindrance to the orator.

Susenbrotus (30)
Scheme. When a peroration is added to a passage without any weight of meaning ... something superfluous.

Peacham (1577, Fii^v)
Scheme. *Perissologia* ... when a clause of no weight is thrown into a construction ... a clogging of speech.
Macrologia, a superfluous addition of one word or more to the end of a construction.

EXAMPLES

Susenbrotus (30)
Carolus Augustus lived and did not die.

Peacham (Fii^v)
The ambassadors peace not being obtained, returned home again from whence they came.
Trapezuntius, Melancthon, Veltkirchius, Sherry, Scaliger, Puttenham, Day

Circumlocutio (Periphrasis)

also known as *circuitio*

Quintilian (VIII, vi, 59ff)
Trope. When we use a number of words to describe something for which one, or at any rate only a few words of description would suffice ... a circuitous mode of speech, frequently used among poets for a decorative effect.

Erasmus (27f)
For plentitude of words. Can be an *antonomasia* with many words . . .
etymologia when we indicate the origin of a name, *notatio* when we
describe anything by its distinctive features . . . or when, instead of a
name, we use a definition.

Scaliger (III, xxxii)
A class of figures. When we replace one thing by many.

Scaliger (III, lxxviii)
Under *eclipsis*. When we go round about our subject with many words
and all that can be understood about it but which is not necessary or
inherent in the subject itself is added.

Scaliger (IV, xxxv)
Scheme. When one thing is described by many words, . . . a highly
ornamental figure.

EXAMPLES

Wilson (176)
Henry the fifth, the most puissant King of England, with seven
thousand men took the French king prisoner with all the flower of
nobility in France.
Such a one defiled his body with such an evil woman.

Peacham (148)
As when for this word philosopher, we say a man studious of wisdom.
(Anger) . . . It is a vehement heat of the mind, which bringeth palenesse
to the countenance, burning to the eyes, and trembling to the parts of
the body.
(Tyrant) . . . an oppressor of the laws and liberties of the commonwealth.

Hoskins (47f)
When they had a while hearkened to the persuasion of sleep.
Mopsa disgraced weeping with her countenance.
Plangus' speech began to be translated into the language of suspicion.

Trapezuntius, Erasmus, Melancthon, Susenbrotus, Sherry, Puttenham, Day

Collatio

Erasmus (31)
For plenitude of words. A form of comparison between two things in which a similitude is developed to a full comparison and a metaphor within this comparison is adapted to it.

Scaliger (III, l)
Under *tractatio*. A comparison between two things with regard to the logical sequence that led up to the comparison. This form of comparison explains why the two are compared, and is concerned particularly with things that are different.

EXAMPLES
Erasmus (31)
As iron glows so he burned with wrath.

Scaliger (III, l)
Æneas is compared with the eagle, as a *pilgrim without wings.*

Collectio

Scaliger (III, xxxii)
Generic term for those figures (tropes and schemes) in which one word has more than one meaning.

Collectio (Syllogismos)

Peacham (179)
Scheme. A form by which the orator amplifieth a matter by conjecture, that is by expressing some signs or circumstances of a matter which circumstances be of three sorts, either going before it, annexed with it, or following after it.

EXAMPLES
Peacham (179)
As the Lord God liveth before whom I stand, there shall be neither dew nor rain these years, but according to my word.

Peacham (180)
And he went forth and wept bitterly. . . . David is described sorrow-
fully bewailing the death of his son Absolon, by which is collected how
dearly he loved him.

Quintilian

Commoratio (Epexergasia)
also known as *immoratio*

Cicero (De Oratore, III, liii, 202)
Scheme. Dwelling upon one point, especially effective in stating a case
or for illuminating and amplifying the facts in the course of a statement,
for making our audience regard the point as important as speech can
make it.

Scaliger (III, xlvi)
Under *tractatio*. This device, by which we make our meaning clear
from a different point of view or set out each different aspect of the
subject, belongs to a full style.

Peacham (152)
Scheme. The point whereon the whole weight of the cause depends.
The orator maketh often recourse thither and repeateth it many times
by variation, . . . either by expressing one thing with many words
or by declaring one thing with diverse members, causes, effects and
reasons.

EXAMPLES

Peacham (152f)
And shall so great a virtue be expelled, and thrust out, banished and
cast away from the city?

Cicero when *Eiutius* could show no cause in his accusation, why *Roscius*
should slay his father, he doth first amplify the wicked fact of parricide
. . . and argueth that without many and great causes, such a wickedness
cannot be committed . . . after this he demandeth the cause why

Roscius should slay his father, which place . . . he tarrieth long in it and very often maketh his return thither, he often demandeth the causes of so great and horrible wickedness.

Ad Herennium, Quintilian
Melancthon, Veltkirchius, Susenbrotus, Wilson, Puttenham, Day

Communicatio (Anachinosis)

Cicero (Orator, xl, 138)
Scheme. When often we almost confer on the matter in hand with those who listen or even with our opponent.

Puttenham (227)
Scheme. To acquaint our judge, hearer or adversary with some part of our counsel and advice and to ask their opinion, as who would say they could not otherwise think of the matter than we do.

EXAMPLES

Wilson (187)
What think you in this matter? Is there any other better means to dispatch the thing? What would you have done, if you were in the same case? Here I appeal to your own conscience, whether you would suffer this unpunished, if a man should do you the like displeasure.

Fraunce (98f)
Shall I say, O *Cleophila*? Alas your words be against it . . . shall I say prince *Pirocles*? Wretch that I am, your shew is manifest against it. . . . Alas what then shall I do? Shall I seek far fetched inventions?

Hoskins (49)
Were it your case, what would you answer? Tell me, I appeal unto your secret thoughts . . . would you not judge him unworthy ever to be your friend that began not his fidelity with an inviolable covenant never to be your enemy?

Quintilian, Rufinianus
Melancthon, Susenbrotus, Talaeus, Sherry, Scaliger, Peacham

Commutatio (Antimetabole)
also known as *antimetathesis, metathesis*

Ad Herennium (IV, 39)
When two discrepant thoughts are so expressed by transposition that the latter follows from the former, although contradictory to it.

Quintilian (IX, iii, 85)
Scheme. Words are repeated in different cases, tenses, moods and so on. ... Again the clauses may end with the same word. A special elegance may be secured by placing names in antithetical positions.

Susenbrotus (82f)
Scheme. A sentence is inverted by becoming its contrary. ... From this scheme enthymemic arguments may be derived. In this way rhetoricians derive an enthymeme from contraries.

Scaliger (III, xxxvii)
Antimetabole. A sentence is changed to its contrary.
Antimetathesis. When we allow words to change places. An opposite meaning may be derived from the transposing of the words.

Puttenham (208)
Scheme. A figure which takes a couple of words to play with in a verse and by making them to change and shift one into others place they do very prettily exchange and shift the sense.

EXAMPLES

Puttenham (209)

> If Poesie be, as some have said,
> A speaking picture to the eye:
> Then is a picture not denied,
> To be a mute Poesie.

Hoskins (15)
If any, for love of honour or honour of love. ...
Parthenia desired above all things to have Argalus; Argalus feared nothing but to miss Parthenia.

Rutilius Lupus
Melancthon, Day, Peacham

Compar (Parison)
also known as *isocolon, exaequatio*

Ad Herennium (IV, 27f)
Scheme. When the different parts of the sentences which make up a speech balance each other by having equal numbers of syllables.

Scaliger (IV, xxxix)
Scheme. In this figure the sections of a passage are balanced by words or sounds always equal in number and length. Used well it is a great virtue of style, badly it may become a vice.

Puttenham (214)
Scheme. It goeth by clauses of equal quantity, and not very long. . . . They give good grace to a ditty, but specially to a prose. . . . . In a prose there should not be used at once of such even clauses past three or four.

Hoskins (37f)
Scheme. An even gait of sentences answering each other in measures interchangeably. . . . Words match each other in rank, verb to verb, adverb to adverb etc.

EXAMPLES

Wilson (204)
Law without mercy, is extreme power, yet men through folly, deserve such justice.

Peacham (59)
He left the city garnished, that the same might be a monument of victory, of clemency, of continency, that men might see, what he had conquered, what he spared, what he had left.
The ox hath known his owner, and the ass his masters crib.

Hoskins (37f)

Such as in St. Augustine but often in Gregory the Divine . . . and many places of *Euphues* . . . do very much mingle this figure with [*alliteratio*] and *similiter cadens* . . . as in, If ever I could wish my faith untried and my counsel untrusted.

Save his gray hairs from rebuke and his aged mind from despair.

Quintilian, Aquila
Sherry

Comparatio (Analogia)

Quintilian (IX, ii, 100)

Scheme. *Comparatio* is regarded as a figure although at times it is a form of proof. . . . I am not sure whether it is so much a scheme of thought as of words. For the only difference lies in the fact that universals are not contrasted with universals, but particulars with particulars.

Quintilian (VIII, iv, 9)

Used for amplification, it seeks to rise from the less to the greater, since by raising what is below it must necessarily exalt that which is above.

Scaliger (III, l)

Under *tractatio*. This figure sets down a known object to which the subject of discourse is compared. . . . We may compare persons, things, times, places, events. . . . Comparison proper always discovers similarity.

Hoskins (17ff)

Comparing things equal, we search out all the points of a consorted equality, . . . with most profit by inventing matter of agreement in things most unlike. . . . Comparing things different . . . it is most commendable where there seems to be great affinity in the matter conferred. . . . Comparison of contraries . . . is by pairs . . . with interchangeable correspondencies in sentences . . . where you may observe every word in the latter sentence aggravated by opposition to every word in the former.

44

EXAMPLES

Peacham (156f)
Camillus by his vertue did drive away the Barbarians and set up again
the Roman Empire: even so *Laurentius Valla* restored the Latin tongue
to the former purity which through the ignorance of the Barbarians
was corrupted.
Brutus put his sons to death, for that they conspired treason: *Manlius*
punished his son for his virtue.
If they have called the master of the house Beelzebub, how much more
them of his household?

Hoskins (20ff)
If to protract battle upon advice be cowardice, then Phocion, then
Metellus, then Fabius, then all the valiantest captains of all ages were
cowards.
He that prefers wealthy ignorance before chargeable study prefers
contempt before honour, darkness before light, death before life, and
earth before heaven.
Did the most innocent vouchsafe it as a part of His glory to pray for
His enemies, and shall we, the most sinful, esteem it a blot to our
reputation to be unrevenged on our brethren?

Cicero
Erasmus, Susenbrotus, Puttenham, Day

Comparatio (Antithesis)
also known as *sygchrisis*

Rufinianus (64)
Scheme. The comparison of persons or things which are in themselves
contrary.

Peacham (162)
Scheme. A comparison of contrary things and diverse persons in one
sentence.

EXAMPLES

Peacham (162)

Behold my servants shall eat, and you shall suffer hunger, behold my servants shall drink, and you shall abide thirst.

We are indeed rightfully here, for we receive things worthy of that we have done, but this man hath done nothing amiss.

Wise women uphold their house, but a foolish woman pulleth it down.

Cicero
Melancthon, Veltkirchius, Sherry

Compensatio (Antenagoge)

also known as *retributio*

Aquila (102ᵛ)

Scheme. Here something difficult or adverse is admitted against our case but is balanced with another fact no less certain.

Scaliger (III, li)

Under *tractatio*. To describe some accusation or action which balances the crime or charge in question when we cannot exculpate our client.

Puttenham (216)

Scheme. Having spoken anything to deprave the matter . . . the speaker denieth it not but . . . helpeth it again by another more favourable speech.

Peacham (93)

Scheme. The speaker joins to a precept of virtue a promise of reward and to the contempt of a precept, he pronounceth a punishment.

EXAMPLES

Puttenham (216)

> My wife is a shrew,
> But such a housewife as I know but a few.

Peacham (93)

If thou shall obey the voice of the Lord thy God, and observe and do all his commandments, which I command thee this day, then the Lord thy God will set thee on high above all the nations of the earth. . . . But if thou wilt not obey the voice of the Lord thy God, to keep and do all his commandments . . . which I command thee this day, then all these curses shall come upon thee, and overtake thee.

Fortunatianus
Day

Complexio (Symploche)
also known as *conduplicatio, comprehensio, circulo rhetorica*

Ad Herennium (IV, 20)
Conplexio. . . . When we repeat both the first word and the last in a succession of phrases.

Fraunce (44)
Scheme. When the same sound is repeated both in beginnings and endings.

Hoskins (13)
When several sentences have the same beginning and the same ending. . . . This is the wantonest of repetitions, and is not to be used in matters too serious.

EXAMPLES

Fraunce (44)
My blood will satisfy the highest point of equity, my blood will satisfy the hardest hearted of this country.
Such was as then the estate of the Duke, as it was no time by direct means to seek her, and such was the estate of his captived will, as he could delay no time of seeking her.

Peacham (43)
Who were they that often broke their leagues? the Carthaginians . . . who were they that made cruel war in Italy? the Carthaginians. . . . Who crave pardon now? the Carthaginians.

Hoskins (13)
The most covetous man longs not to get riches out of a ground which

47

can bear nothing. Why? Because it is impossible. The most ambitious wight vexeth not his wits to climb into heaven. Why? because it is impossible.

Aquila
Melancthon, Susenbrotus, Talaeus, Sherry, Wilson, Scaliger, Puttenham, Day

Compositio (Synthesis)

Ad Herennium (IV, 18)
An arrangement of words which gives uniform polish to the discourse in every part. To ensure this virtue we shall avoid the frequent collision of vowels ... excessive recurrence of the same letter ... and excessive repetition of the same word or case ending.

Scaliger (III, xl)
Scheme. To permit a particular metrical arrangement, one word is squeezed together out of two words, as in multiple-dithyrambics. This is usually done with the diction of a lower style.

EXAMPLES

Ad Herennium (IV, 18)
Bacae aeneae amoenissime independebant.

Scaliger (III, xl)
Antemalorum. Semperflorentis, after Lucretius.

Melancthon, Veltkirchius

Comprehensio (Periodos)
also known as *continuatio*

Ad Herennium (IV, 27)
A close-packed and uninterrupted group of words embracing a complete thought. We shall best use it in three places: in a maxim, in a contrast and in a conclusion.

48

Scaliger (IV, xxv)
Scheme. The period contains a complete idea. Brief ideas are naturally unsuited to a periodic structure. . . . According to Aristotle a period is a unit that contains the beginning and end of its statement within itself.

EXAMPLE

Veltkirchius (37)
Those who till the soil, navigate the seas, and raise buildings display all the capacities of man.

Cicero, Quintilian

Comprobatio
also known as *conciliatio* (not to be confused with *paradiastole*)

Wilson (200)
Scheme. Sometimes we seek favour by speaking well of the company present.

Peacham (1577, H$_v$)
Scheme. When we see some good thing either in the judges or in the hearers or in any other. And therefore declare we do well allow of it, and also commend them for it.

EXAMPLES

Wilson (200)
Through your help my Lords, this good deed hath been done.

Peacham (H$_v$)
I commend and praise you, you Judges, for that most lovingly ye do advance the name of so famous a young man. Also believe me, you have done well in punishing so wicked a wretch, for now others may take example by him, also, God grant you may proceed in this your well doing.

Melancthon

Conceptio (Syllepsis)
also known as *adjunctio*

Scaliger (III, lxxvii)
Under *eclipsis*. By a number of singulars this figure signifies a multitude, under one genus it comprehends others ... that is, two things are signified by the one word.

Puttenham (165f)
A word wanting in sundry clauses *and of several congruities or sense* [cf. ADJUNCTIO—this is the difference], and the supply be made to serve them all ... conceiving and as it were comprehending under one, a supply of two natures.

EXAMPLES
Puttenham (165f)

> Here my sweet sons and daughters all my bliss,
> Yonder mine own dear husband buried is.

> Judge I ye lovers, if it be strange or no:
> My lady laughs for joy, and I for woe.

> Thus valiantly and with a manly mind,
> And by one feat of everlasting fame,
> This lusty lad fully requited kind,
> His father's death and eke his mother's shame.

Quintilian, Rufinianus
Melancthon, Veltkirchius, Susenbrotus, Sherry, Day

Concessio (Epitrope)
also known as *permissio*

Ad Herennium (IV, 39)
When we openly say that we voluntarily give away or concede the whole matter to another's will.

Scaliger (III, lvii)
Under *tractatio*. When we grant the part of our case we cannot defend, and then leave it.

Fraunce (104f)
Scheme. When we jestingly admit of any speech or argument ... delighteth much when we grant that which hurteth him to whom it is granted.

Peacham (112)
Scheme. The speaker granteth something ironically ... meaning an earnest forbidding though the words be otherwise.

EXAMPLES
Fraunce (104)
But yet even of favour, let us grant him thus much more, as to fancy, that in these foretold things, fortune might be a great actor, perchance to an an evil end, yet to a less evil end, all these intangled devices were intended.

Peacham (112)
Rejoice, O young man in thy youth, and let thy heart cheer thee in thy young days, and walk in the ways of thine own heart, and in the sight of thine eyes: but know thou, that for all these things God will bring thee into judgment.

Hoskins (50)
I admit you are resolute; I grant your determination is immoveable; but it is in things against your friend's judgment, and things against your own praise and profit.

Quintilian, Rufinianus
Melancthon, Susenbrotus, Talaeus, Sherry, Puttenham, Day

Conciliatio (Paradiastole)
also known as *substitutio*

Quintilian (IX, ii, 92)
Scheme. Those figures by means of which we give gentle expression

to unpleasing facts. . . . All such devices which consist in saying one think while intending something else to be understood, have a strong resemblance to allegory.

Peacham (1577, H_v^v)
Scheme. When by a mannerly interpretation we excuse our own vices or other men's . . . by calling them virtues. . . . This figure is used when vices are excused.

Puttenham (184f)
Scheme. If a moderation of words tend to flattery or to soothing or excusing . . . to turn a signification to the more plausible sense . . . moderating and abating the force of the matter by craft, and for a pleasing purpose.

Peacham (168)
Vice. It opposeth the truth by false terms and wrong names.

EXAMPLES

Peacham (H_v^v)
When we call him that is crafty, wise: a covetous man, a good husband: murder a manly deed: deep dissimulation, singular wisdom: pride cleanliness: covetousness, a worldly or necessary carefulness: whoredom, youthful delight and dalliance: idolatory, pure religion.

Peacham (168)
In calling drunkeness good fellowship, insatiable avarice good husbandry, craft and deceit wisdom and policy.

Puttenham (185)
For a great riot, a youthful prank.

Cicero, Rutilius Lupus, Rufinianus
Melancthon, Wilson, Scaliger, Day

Conclusio (Epilogos)

Ad Herennium (IV, 41)
Scheme. A brief argument which deduces from the preceding facts and sayings the necessary conclusions.

Wilson (183)
Scheme. An apt knitting together of that which we have said before.

Peacham (1577, Mii^v)
Scheme. By a brief argumentation concludes necessarily upon that, which is said or done before.

EXAMPLES

Wilson (183)
If reason can persuade, if examples may move, if necessity may help, if pity may provoke, if dangers forseen may stir us to be wise: I doubt not but you will rather use sharp laws to repress offenders, than with dissolute negligence suffer all to perish.

Peacham (Mii^v)
First you must needs confess your own faults, before you can rebuke or control any faults of Ligarius.
For if it be shewed by reason and proved by example, that we ought to venture in jeopardy and peril for the commonwealth, they are to be counted wise men which do shun no danger for the safeguard of their country.

Cicero, Quintilian
Sherry

Confessio (Paramologia)
also known as *paralogia*

Quintilian (IX, ii, 17)
Scheme. One of the species of the genus *prolepsis* [see under PRAE-SUMPTIO], a form of confession where [Cicero] admits he regards his client as worthy of censure for lending money to the king.

Puttenham (227)
Scheme. When all that should seem to make against him . . . he should admit . . . confess and avoid.

Peacham (173f)
Scheme. When the speaker granteth many things to his adversary worthy of commendation, and at length bringeth in some notable crime, which oppresseth and quencheth all that was granted before. . . . When the speaker in his conclusion bringeth in that which was not looked for, or that which is contrary or at least far distant from the premises.

EXAMPLES
Peacham (173f)
Notwithstanding this I say concerning the whole nation of the Greeks, I grant unto them learning, I grant unto them knowledge of many arts, I take not from them the comely grace of speech, fine wits, singular eloquence. And furthermore, if they challenge unto themselves any other thing, I will not deny it them, yet religion and faith that nation never favoured.
Solomon rehearseth the parts of his felicity, he mentioneth his riches, possessions, sumptuous buildings and pleasures: but suddenly he concludeth that all this is but vanity and vexation of spirit.

Rutilius Lupus
Melancthon, Susenbrotus, Wilson, Scaliger, Day

Conformatio (Prosopopoeia)
also known as *attributio, personae ficta, prosopographia*

Quintilian (VIII, vi, 11)
Trope. Effects of extraordinary sublimity are produced when the theme is exalted by a bold and almost hazardous metaphor and inanimate objects are given life and action.

Quintilian (IX, ii, 29ff)
Scheme. *Fictiones personarum* or *prosopopoeia*. . . . We display the inner thoughts of our adversaries as though they were talking with ourselves . . . or . . . we may introduce conversations bet weenourselves and others . . . we are even allowed in this manner of speaking to bring

down the gods from heaven and raise the dead, while cities and peoples may also find a voice. ... I have included both *prosopopoeia* and *dialogismos* (*sermocinatio*) under the same generally accepted term since we cannot imagine a speech without imagining also a person to utter it. ... We lend a voice to things to which nature has denied it. ... Again, we often personify the abstract as Virgil does with Fame.

Scaliger (III, xlviii)
Under *tractatio*. If mute things are addressed, if speech is attributed to mute things, if not speech but sense is attributed to things without sense, if intelligence is assigned to the non-intelligent or to the half-intelligent such as animals, we have *prosopopoeia*. This figure includes fictive persons such as Fame and the Furies, and things with human properties attributed to them. ... All these beings are always invented.

Puttenham (239)
Scheme. If ye will feign any person with such features, qualities and conditions, or if ye will attribute any human quality, as reason or speech, to dumb creatures or other insensible things and do study to give them a human person ... by way of fiction.

Hoskins (48)
To animate and give life. ... To make dead men speak. ... Sir Philip Sidney gives meaning and speech to the needle, the cloth and the silk; as learning, as a city, as death itself is feigned to live and make a speech.

EXAMPLES

Fraunce (91f)
Arcadia finding herself in these desolate terms, doth speak ... so unfortunately, that it doth appal her mind though she had leisure.

Peacham (136)
He may after he hath sufficiently praised truth feign it a person and bring it in bitterly complaining how cruelly she is oppressed and how little esteemed, ... he may feign her complaining against false balances, ... against fear, favour and avarice which are her enemies in the seats of judgment conspiring against her and violently throwing her down from thence.

E

Hoskins (48)
If your ancestors were now alive and saw you defacing so goodly a principality by them established, would they not say thus?

*Ad Herennium, Cicero, Rutilius Lupus, Aquila, Rufinianus
Erasmus, Melancthon, Susenbrotus, Talaeus, Sherry, Day*

Confusio (Synchysis)

Susenbrotus (33)
Scheme. By this figure the order of all parts of any passage is disarranged and confused.

Peacham (1577, Gi)
Vice. A confusion of order in all parts of the construction ... it is unprofitable, and rather to be avoided, than at any time to be imitated.

EXAMPLE
Peacham (Gi)
The wines good which afterward had in pipes laid aboard *Acestes* on *Sicilian* shore, and given to the Trojans departing, the noble man did distribute.

Congeries (Synathrismos)
also known as *coagmentatio, cumulatio, accumulatio, coacervatio, symphoresis*

Quintilian (VIII, iv, 26f)
Under *amplificatio*. An accumulation of words and sentences with the same meaning. Although the climax is not in this case reached by a series of steps it is none the less attained by the piling up of words. It resembles the figure *synathrismos* in which a number of different things are accumulated, but in *congeries* proper all the accumulated words have but one meaning.

Susenbrotus (71)
Scheme. This figure is the enumeration of words which signify various different things. It differs from *synonymia* [see under INTERPRETATIO]

by which one thing is expressed in many different words or phrases of the same meaning: *congeries* is an accumulation of many things.

Scaliger (III, xliii)
Under *tractatio*. *Coagmentatio*: this figure heaps things up in order to incite to action. It is stylistically more elevated than *acervatio*.

Scaliger (III, xlvi)
Under *tractatio*. *Accumulatio*: this figure simply accumulates and like *acervatio* belongs to a lower style.

Puttenham (236)
Scheme. To be earnest. .... we lay on such load and so go to it by heaps as if we would win the game by multitude of words and speeches, not all of one but of diverse matters and sense.

EXAMPLES
Puttenham (236)
But if my faith, my hope, my love, my true intent. . . .

Peacham (132)
Thus all things were mixed together with blood, manslaughter, theft and deceit, corruption, and unfaithfulness, sedition, perjury, disquieting of good men, unthankfulness, defiling of souls, changing of birth, disorder in marriage, adultery and uncleanness.

Hoskins (25)
He hath a sweet countenance, a most pleasant eye, a most amiable presence, a cheerful aspect; he is a most delectable object.

Hoskins (31)
Love's companions be unquietness, longings, fond comforts, faint discomforts, hopes, jealousies, ungrounded rages, causeless yieldings. Spite, rage, disdain, shame, revenge came upon hatred.

Rutilius Lupus
Trapezuntius, Erasmus, Melancthon, Susenbrotus, Day

Conglobatio (Systrophe)
also known as *convolutio*

Peacham (153)
Scheme. Bringeth in many definitions of one thing yet not such definitions as do declare the substance of a thing by the kind and the difference, which the art of reasoning doth prescribe, but by others of another kind all heaped together.

EXAMPLES

Peacham (153)
An history is the testimony of times, the light of verity, the maintenance of memory, the schoolmistress of life, and messenger of antiquity.
Man is the example of imbecility, the image of unconstancy, the spoil of time, the bondman of misery, the vessel of insatiable desire, and the confident castle of sudden ruin.
Pleasures are the enemies of chastity, guides to poverty, daughters of dishonesty, and sweet baits of extreme misery.

Trapezuntius

Consolatio (Paramythia)

Scaliger (III, cxxiii)
Under *adhortatio*. This kind of speech brings the soul of the listener to tranquillity. If we make the stature of our subject less, the listener is drawn to pity; if greater, to acceptance; if equal, to friendship.

Peacham (100)
Scheme. A form of speech which the orator useth to take away or diminish a sorrow conceived in the mind of his hearer.

EXAMPLES

Peacham (100)
> O mates (quoth he) that many a woe have bid, and born ere this,
> Worse have we seen, and these also shall end, when Gods will is.
Blessed is the man whom God correcteth, therefore refuse not thou the

chastening of the almighty, for he maketh the wound and bindeth it up, he smiteth and his hand maketh whole.

Cicero

Constantia (Eustathia)

Peacham (69f)
Scheme. The orator or speaker promiseth and protesteth his constancy concerning something. . . . To declare the firm and unremovable purpose of the mind. . . . By contempt of torture and death itself, by comparison of impossibilities.

EXAMPLES

Peacham (69)
Let lion's claws tear out our bowels, let the gibbet hang us, let the fire consume us, let the sword cut us asunder, let wild beasts tread us under their feet: yet we Christians are by prayer prepared to abide all pain and torments.
I am persuaded that neither death, nor life, nor angels, nor principalities, nor powers, neither things present, nor things to come, neither height, nor depth, nor any other creature shall be able to separate us from the love of God, which is in Christ Jesus our Lord.

> The fish shall fly the flood, the serpent bide the fire,
> Ere ever I for gain or good will alter my desire.

Constructio (Syntaxis)

Erasmus (37)
For plenitude of words. Some variety in speech comes from syntax . . . from expressions that admit of different constructions.

EXAMPLES

Erasmus (37)
Much modesty, much of modesty.
The whole night long, throughout the night.

Consummatio (Diallage)

Quintilian (IX, ii, 103)
Scheme. When a number of different arguments are used to establish one point.

Quintilian (IX, iii, 49)
A mixture of words, some identical and others different in meaning.

Scaliger (III, lxiv)
Under *tractatio*. When many arguments tend to one end.

EXAMPLE
Quintilian (IX, iii, 49)
I ask my enemies whether these plots were investigated, discovered and laid bare, overthrown, crushed and destroyed by me.

Contentio (Antitheton)

also known as *repugnantia, contrapositum* (not to be confused with *syneciosis*)

Quintilian (IX, iii, 81f)
Scheme. Single words may be contrasted with single, . . . or the contrast may be between pairs of words . . . or sentence may be contrasted with sentence. . . . Nor is the contrasted phrase always placed immediately after that to which it is opposed . . . but . . . we may have correspondence between subsequent particulars and others previously mentioned.

Wilson (199)
Scheme. Contrariety, is when our talk standeth by contrary words or sentences together.

Scaliger (IV, xxxvii)
Scheme. The contrast here is not merely between different words but between the ideas they convey. . . . It is a most elegant form of speech, putting in first something like and then something unlike.

Hoskins (37)
An opposition of terms disagreeing . . . respecting the contrarieties of
things meant thereby.

EXAMPLES

Wilson (199f)
To his friend he is churlish, to his foe he is gentle: give him fair words
and you offend him: check him sharply and you win him. Let him have
his will, and he will fly in thy face: keep him short and you shall have
him at commandment.

Puttenham (210)
> His bent is sweet, his loose is somewhat sour,
> In joy begun, ends oft in woeful hour.

Hoskins (37)
There was strength against nimbleness, rage against resolution, fury
against virtue, confidence against courage, pride against nobleness.
He is a swaggerer amongst quiet men, but a quiet man amongst
swaggerers; earnest in idle things, idle in matters of earnestness.

Ad Herennium, Cicero, Aquila, Rufinianus
Erasmus, Melancthon, Susenbrotus, Sherry, Day, Peacham

Contrapositum (Syneciosis)
also known as *conjunctio, commistio*

Susenbrotus (82)
Scheme. In this figure a contrary is joined to its opposite or, in other
words, two different things are closely conjoined.

Puttenham (206)
Scheme. Takes . . . two contrary words and tieth them together.

Hoskins (36)
Scheme. A composition of contraries, and by both words imitateth
the meaning of neither precisely but a moderation and mediocrity of
both; as, *bravery* and *rags* are contrary, yet somewhat better than both

61

is *brave raggedness* ... one contrary is affirmed to be in the other directly by making one the substantive, the other the adjective.

EXAMPLES

Peacham (170)
Gluttonous feasting and starving famine all are one, for both weaken the body, procure sickness, and cause death.

Puttenham (207)
> Thus for your sake I daily die,
> And do but seem to live in deed:
> Thus is my bliss but misery.

Hoskins (36)
And with that, she prettily smiled, which, mingled with her tears, a man could not tell whether it were mourning pleasure or delightful sorrow.
Seeking honour by dishonouring and building safety upon ruin.

Cicero, Quintilian
Melancthon, Scaliger, Day

Contrarium (Enthymema)
also known as *antithesis, oppositio*

Quintilian (VIII, v, 9f)
Enthymeme ... in its strict sense means a *sententia* drawn from contraries ... it may sometimes be employed for the purpose of ornament.

Scaliger (III, lxi)
Under *tractatio*. An incomplete syllogism in which one of the two premises is suppressed or is expressed as part of the conclusion.

Peacham (162)
Scheme. A form of speech which Quintilian interpreteth a comment forasmuch as it may well be called the whole action and sentence of the mind as it is ... when the sentence concluded consisteth of contraries.

EXAMPLES

Peacham (162f)
Our elders made war, not only that they might be free, but also that
they might rule: but thou thinkest war may be left off, that we might
be made bondslaves to serve.
They which may do me good, will not, and they which are willing,
cannot, therefore my distress remaineth.

Ad Herennium, Rufinianus, Fortunatianus

Conversio (Antistrophe)
also known as *epiphora, epistrophe* (not to be confused with *inversio*).

Ad Herennium (IV, 19)
When we repeat that last word of successive phrases.

Susenbrotus (51)
Scheme. When several phrases in succession end with the same word.

Fraunce (42)
Scheme. When the like sound is iterated in the endings.

EXAMPLES

Fraunce (43)
O no, he can not be good, that knows not why he is good, but stands
so far good as his fortune may keep him unassailed.

Puttenham (199)
> But seeing her love so lightly won and lost:
> I longed not for her love, for well I thought,
> Firm is the love, if it be as it ought.

Hoskins (13)
Where the richness did invite the eyes, the fashion did entertain the
eyes, and the device did teach the eyes.
Either arm their lives or take away their lives.

Cicero, Aquila, Rufinianus
Trapezuntius, Melancthon, Talaeus, Sherry, Wilson, Scaliger, Day,
Peacham

Copulatio (Ploche)
also known as *conduplicatio, diacope*

Ad Herennium (IV, 38)
Scheme. When one or more words are iterated for the purpose of amplifying our subject or drawing forth feelings of commiseration. . . . This vehement way of speaking makes a deep impression on the feelings of the audience.

Puttenham (201)
Scheme. A speedy iteration of one word but with some little intermission by inserting one or two words between.

Peacham (48)
Scheme. A figure which repeateth a word putting but one word in between, or at least very few. . . . May be used to express any affection, but it is most fit for a sharp invective or exprobation . . . and also an apt ornament for meditation.

EXAMPLES
Puttenham (202)
> Yet when I saw myself to you was true
> I loved myself, because myself loved you.

Peacham (48)
My heart is fixed, O God, my heart is fixed.

Thou art my portion, O God, thou art my portion. I have sinned, O thou maker of men, I have sinned, and what shall I do?

Quintilian, Aquila, Rufinianus
Melancthon, Veltkirchius, Scaliger, Fraunce, Day

Correctio (Epanorthosis)

also known as *metanoia, moderatio, commutatio* (not be confused with *antimetabole*)

Cicero (*Orator*, xxxix, 135)
Scheme. We may correct ourselves, giving an apparent censure of our carelessness.

Talaeus (79f)
Scheme. When we restate something we have said before. By this we revise either what was said or our means of saying it and express our repentance.

Puttenham (215)
Scheme. When we speak and are sorry for it . . . so that we seem to call in our word again and to put in another fitter for the purpose.

Hoskins (29f)
Means of *amplificatio.* Having used a word of sufficient force, yet pretending a greater vehemence of meaning, refuseth it and supplies the place with a greater . . . used when you would make the thing more credible itself than in the manner of your utterance.

EXAMPLES

Wilson (186)
We have brought before you my Lords . . . not a thief, but an extortioner and violent robber, not an adulterer, but a ravisher of maids, not a stealer of church goods, but an errant traitor, both to God and all godliness.

Fraunce (79)
In *Thessalia* I say there was (well I may say there was) a prince: no, no prince, whom bondage wholly possessed, but yet accounted a prince and named *Musidorus.*

Hoskins (29f)
I persuaded you not to lose hold of occasion whilst it may not only be taken but offers, nay, sues to be taken.

65

You stars, you do not succour me! No, no you will not help me!
O Parthenia! No more Parthenia! What art thou?

Ad Herennium, Quintilian, Rufinianus
Trapezuntius, Erasmus, Melancthon, Susenbrotus, Scaliger, Day, Peacham

Cumulatio (Sardismos)
also known as *soraismos*

Quintilian (VIII, iii, 59)
Vice. Consists in the indiscriminate use of several different dialects. . . .
A similar fault is found . . . consisting in the indiscriminate mixture of
grand words with mean, old with new, and poetic with colloquial.

Puttenham (252)
Vice. When we make our speech or writings of sundry languages . . .
not for the nonce or for any purpose (which were in part excusable)
but ignorantly and affectedly.

Peacham (1577, Giv)
Vice. A mingling together of diverse languages, as when there is one
sentence English, Latin and French.

EXAMPLES

Quintilian (VIII, iii, 59)
As would result from mixing Doric, Ionic and even Aeolic words with
Attic.

Puttenham (253)
And of an ingenious invention infanted by pleasant travail (from *enfant*).
I will freddon in thine honour (from *freddon*).

Veltkirchius, Sherry

Defectio (Ellipsis)
Quintilian (VIII, vi, 21)
Vice. When something is assumed which has not actually been ex-
pressed. When such an omission creates a blemish it is called an *ellipsis*.

Scaliger (IV, xxvii)
Scheme. When in an extreme indication of emotion words fail us,
thus giving expression to admiration, love, hate, anger. *Ellipsis* of a
word may lead to ineptness of expression. . . . Rare in the poets but
used often in comedy.

EXAMPLE

Scaliger (IV, xxvii)
S'ein quomodo?

Aquila, Fortunatianus
Melancthon

Definitio (Orismos)
also known as *circumscriptio, finitio, catadiaphora*

Ad Herennium (IV, 35)
Each thing is described with its own proper attributes in a brief and
clear fashion. . . . It sets forth the full meaning and character of a
thing so lucidly and briefly that to express it in more words seems
superfluous, and in fewer impossible.

Peacham (128)
Scheme. The orator declareth the proper pith of some thing, and it is
chiefly used, when there is a difference sought for between two words
which by defining this findeth forth . . . to distinguish between two
words or matter of nigh affinity or to separate one thing from another.

Hoskins (43f)
The shortest and truest exposition of the nature of anything. . . . Your
definitions need not be strictly tied to the rules of logic.

EXAMPLES

Wilson (208)
He is free that is subject to no evil.

67

Peacham (128)

This is not fortitude but temerity, for fortitude is a contempt of perils by honest reason: temerity is a foolish enterprise of perils without respect of virtue.

For neither is this to be counted thy life, which is contained in thy body and breath, but that is thy life . . . which shall live and flourish in memory unto the worlds end, which posterity shall nourish, which eternity shall ever behold.

To refuse good counsel is folly, to condemn it is wickedness, to scorn it is madness.

Hoskins (44)

Fear is an apprehension of future harm.

Thrift is a moderate and lawful increase of wealth by careful government of your own estate.

Compliment is performance of affected ceremonies in words, looks or gesture.

Cicero, Rutilius Lupus
Melancthon, Susenbrotus, Sherry, Scaliger, Puttenham, Day

Dementiens (Hyperbole)
also known as *superlatio, audacia*

Quintilian (VIII, vi, 67ff)

Trope. An elegant straining of the truth which may be employed either for exaggeration or attenuation. . . . We may say more than the actual facts. . . . We may exalt our theme by the use of simile . . . or by the introduction of a comparison . . . or by a metaphor . . . one *hyperbole* may be heightened by the addition of another . . . *Hyperbole* lies without any intention to deceive. . . . When the magnitude of the facts passes all words our language will be more effective if it goes beyond the truth than if it falls short of it.

Erasmus (35)

For plenitude of words. A means of variation. By this lie Seneca says we come to truth . . . in that what is true is understood from the false.

Talaeus (4f)
Trope. By far the greatest ornament when one such trope is joined to and continues after another, which continuation, if consistent, we call allegory.

Scaliger (III, xxxii)
A generic term for that group of figures by which more is signified than in reality exists.

Hoskins (29)
Means of *amplificatio*. Sometimes it expresseth a thing to the highest degree of possibility beyond the truth, that it descending thence may find the truth; sometimes in flat impossibility, that rather you may conceive the unspeakableness than the untruth of the relation.

EXAMPLES

Wilson (183)
God promised to Abraham, that he would make his posterity equal with the sands of the earth.
He hath a belly as big as a barrel.

Fraunce (19)
But, alas, to what a sea of miseries my plentiful tongue doth lead me?
She that could before scarce go, but supported by crutches, now flew about the house born up by the wings of anger.

Hoskins (29)
Accustomed to use victory as an inheritance.
Though a thousand deaths followed, and every death followed with a hundred shames.
Beyond the bounds of conceit, much more of uttering.

Ad Herennium, Cicero
Melancthon, Susenbrotus, Sherry, Puttenham, Day, Peacham

Demonstratio (Hypotyposis)
also known as *suffiguratio, evidentia, effictio* (not to be confused with *prosographia*)

Ad Herennium (IV, 68)

This figure so explains things with words that we apprehend them as though before our eyes. We bring this about by describing what the thing has done, does and will do, the circumstances and consequences of its existence.

Erasmus (47f)

For exposition. When we enrich our speech by the description of a thing, when we . . . place it before the reader painted with all the colours of rhetoric . . . This figure consists chiefly in the exposition of details.

Susenbrotus (86)

Scheme. When we describe anything in order that our hearers might seem to see it before them. . . . It may be used to amplify our subject, to adorn it or to delight the audience by the beauty of our description. The following schemes are forms of *demonstratio: effictio, conformatio, descriptio, locus, topothesia* and *tempus.*

Puttenham (238)

Scheme. To describe and set forth many things in such sort as it should appear they were truly before our eyes . . . if these things . . . be not natural or not veritable, the same asketh more cunning because to feign a thing that never was nor is like to be proceedeth of a greater wit and sharper invention than to describe things that be true.

EXAMPLE

Wilson (178)

If our enemies shall invade, and by treason win the victory, we all shall die . . . and our city shall be destroyed stick and stone. I see our children made slaves, our daughters ravished, our wives carried away, the father forced to kill his own son, the mother her daughter . . . the sucking child slain in the mother's bosom, one standing to the knees in another's blood, churches spoiled, houses plucked down, and all set in fire round about us.

Cicero, Quintilian
Melancthon, Sherry, Scaliger, Day

Deprecatio
Ad Herennium (I, 24)

When the defendant confesses both crime and premeditation, yet begs for compassion.

Cicero (*De Oratore*, III, liii, 205)
Scheme. Entreaty.

EXAMPLE
Ad Herennium (I, 24)
Even if he had done this, it would still be more appropriate to pardon him in view of his past services; but he does not at all beg for pardon.

Descriptio (Pragmatographia)

Ad Herennium (IV, 51)
The figure which contains a clear, lucid and impressive exposition of the consequences of an act.

Puttenham (239f)
Scheme. The counterfeit action . . . such descriptions be made to represent the handling of any business with the circumstances belonging thereunto . . . battle, feast, marriage, burial.

Peacham (139)
Scheme. A description of things whereby the orator by gathering together all the circumstances belonging to them, doth as plainly portray their image, as if they were most lively painted out in colours and set forth to be seen.

EXAMPLES
Peacham (139f)
If thou wilt open and set abroad all things and every particular . . . there shall appear many fires and scattered flames upon houses and temples, the noise of houses falling down, a confused sound of many things, and woeful cries, some flying . . . others embracing their friends and bidding

F
71

them farewell for ever, infants shrieking, women most bitterly weeping
. . . the spoiling of temporal and profaning of hallowed things. . . .
King *Aeacus* (in 7th book of *Metamorphoses*) maketh a pitiful description of a great and cruel pestilence.
Likewise in the 8th book of the hunting of the wild boar.
Many like descriptions are in Virgil's *Aeneiados:* Cicero describeth the
murdering of *Roscius*, the luxury and riots of *Antony* with many
other more.

Cicero, Quintilian, Fortunatianus
Susenbrotus, Scaliger

Detractio (Eclipsis)

Quintilian (IX, iii, 58f)
Scheme. When the word omitted may be clearly gathered from the
context. . . . Of a similar kind . . . are those passages in which words
are decently omitted to spare our modesty . . . only one word and that
of obvious character is missing.

Scaliger (III, lxxvii)
A generic term for that group of figures by which less is said than the
matter seems to warrant. . . . These figures may be extremely moving.

Puttenham (163)
Scheme. If but one word or some little portion of speech be wanting,
it may be supplied by ordinary understanding.

EXAMPLES
Puttenham (163)
So early a man? (for *Are ye so early a man?*)
I thank God I am to live like a gentleman (for *I am able to live*).

Cicero
Melancthon, Susenbrotus, Sherry, Day

Dictu commoratio (Apomnemonsysis)
also known as *dictu memorabilis*

Robortellus (48ᵛ)
The recitation of a memorable saying or oracle . . . from Demetrius
Phalaerus.

Peacham (87)
Scheme. It is a form of speech by which the orator reciteth some
saying or sentence of another wholly worthy of remembrance and
observation.

EXAMPLES
Peacham (87f)
Hypocrites *Esay* prophesied well of you, saying: This people draweth
near unto me with their mouth and honoureth me with their lips, but
their heart is far from me.
For in him we live and move and have our being, as certain of your
own poets have said, for we are also his generation.

Digressio (Parecbasis)
also known as *excursus, egressio*

Cicero (*De Oratore*, III, liii, 203)
Scheme. We may employ digressions and then, after thus delighting
our audience, make a neat and elegant return to our main theme.

Erasmus (55f)
For plenitude of matter. A discussion departing from the main subject
but still pertinent and useful. . . . To praise, censure, adorn, charm or
prepare for something that follows . . . longer . . . at the beginning of
the speech . . . or at the end.

Scaliger (III, lxxv)
Under *hyperbole*. When something outside the argument is added: thus
we go beyond the original plan of the passage.

Peacham (154)
Scheme. The handling of some matter going out from order but yet for the profit of some pertinent cause, we may digress for the cause of praising, dispraising, delighting or preparing ... necessary ... to see some cause why we should digress.

EXAMPLES

Wilson (181)
I might declare by the way of digression, what a noble country England is, how great commodities it hath, what traffic here is used, and how much more need other realms have of us, than we have need of them. When I shall . . . declaim against an heinous murderer, I may digress from the offence done, and enter in praise of the dead man . . . that the offence done, may be thought so much the greater, the more honest he was, that hath thus been slain.

Peacham (154)
Digressions are taken either from the declaration of deeds, the descriptions of persons, places and times, the reporting of apologies [fables] and similitudes.

Quintilian
Susenbrotus, Puttenham, Day

Dinumeratio (Eutrepismos)
also known as *ordinatio*

Cicero (*De Oratore*, III, liv, 207)
Scheme. To divide and set out under headings.

Wilson (206f)
Scheme. Reckoning is when many things are numbered together. . . .
By this figure we may enlarge that, by rehearsing of the parts, which was spoken generally, and in few words.

Peacham (129)
Scheme. Doth not only number the parts before they be said, but also doth also order those parts, and maketh them plain by a kind of definition, or declaration.

EXAMPLES

Wilson (207)

Look what inheritance came to him . . . by the death of his own kin, and his wife's kinfolk: What dower soever he had by marriage of his wife, which by report was a very great thing: Whatsoever he got by executorship: Whatsoever the King's Majesty gave him. . . . look what money he had, what plate, what apparel, what household stuff, what land and lordships, what sheep, goods, parks, and meadows . . . he hath so spent . . . among the beastly company of filthy queans, among abominable harlots.

Peacham (129f)

There be three things which men do greatly covet, and earnestly follow, riches, pleasures and honours, riches are the nurses of sin and iniquity, pleasures are the daughters of dishonesty, and guides which lead to misery: Honours are mothers and nurses of worldly pomp, and vanity.

Quintilian

Dirimens copulatio

Peacham (171)

Scheme. When we bring forth one sentence with an exception before it, and immediately join another after it that seemeth greater . . . increases the signification by placing the meaner first and the worthier last.

EXAMPLES

Peacham (171)

You have not only taken away my calamity, but also seem to augment my dignity.

Wherefore you must needs obey, not only for fear of vengeance, but also for conscience sake.

Behold, I have not laboured for myself only, but for all them that seek wisdom.

Trapezuntius

Disjunctio (Hypozeuxis)
also known as *diazeugma*

Quintilian (IX, iii, 45)
Scheme. The beginnings and the conclusions of sentences are made to correspond by the use of other words with the same meaning. . . . Some call this *synonymia*, others *disjunctio*: both terms despite their difference, are correct, for the words are differentiated but their meaning is identical.

Puttenham (166)
If the same word supplies sundry clauses or to one clause sundry times iterated and, by several words, so as every clause has his own supply.

Peacham (59f)
Scheme. Joineth to everything a due verb which is contrary to *zeugma* [see under ADJUNCTIO] . . . it is fit for great causes, not withstanding it may be used in others also.

EXAMPLE
Peacham (60)
Such is mans depraved nature and perverse inclination, that taking away the use of government, every kind of evil shall quickly oppress every part of goodness, ambition shall strive for honour, pride shall obtain obedience, malice proceed to murder, . . . whereupon it ensueth that open rebellion is raised, good men murdered, virgins deflowered, holy places polluted, houses burned, cities defaced, laws despised, the whole earth confounded and the omnipotent power of God either little regarded or utterly forgotten.

Ad Herennium, Cicero, Aquila, Rufinianus
Trapezuntius, Melancthon, Sherry

Dissectio (Tmesis)
also known as *sectio, diacope*

Susenbrotus (33)
Scheme. When one expression is divided into two, and one or more words are inserted between the two parts.

Peacham (1577, F$_{iv}$^{v})
Scheme. When a compound word is parted by the intervention of another word and sometimes of many.

EXAMPLES

Peacham (F$_{iv}$^{v})
You rise I perceive early up in a morning (*rise up* parted).
What matters soever (*whatsoever* parted).
My days pass very speedily over (*passover* parted).

Sherry, Scaliger, Day

Dissimilitudo

Peacham (160)
Scheme. Compareth diverse things in a diverse quality . . . to amplify, praise or dispraise, reprehend and confute.

EXAMPLES

Peacham (160)
If we have any disease in our bodies, we use exercise and all other means that we may henceforward be delivered and free from it, but being sick in soul, we dissemble and make delay.
The ox hath known his owner and the ass his masters crib: but Israel hath not known, my people hath taken no heed.
The foxes have holes, and the fowls of the air have nests, but the son of man hath not where to lay his head.

Cicero

Dissimulatio (Mycterismos)

Quintilian (VIII, vi, 59)
Trope. Mockery in which the element of derision is not hid.

Susenbrotus (15f)
Trope. Mockery which is veiled but not suppressed . . . and is usually displayed by gesture rather than word.

Wilson (184)

Scheme. When in words we speak one thing, and mean in heart another thing, declaring either by our countenance or by utterance . . . what our whole meaning is.

Peacham (38f)

Trope. A privy kind of mock . . . yet not so privy but that it may well be perceived. . . . This figure must not be too obscure and dark.

EXAMPLES

Wilson (184f)

When we see one boasting himself . . . to hold him up with yea and nay, and ever to add more to that which he saieth . . . one that said himself to be . . . one of the best in all England for trying of metals. . . . 'Indeed,' said another 'England had a sore loss if God should call you . . . your cunning was such that you brought a shilling to ninepence, nay to sixpence and a groat to twopence'.

Peacham (39)

To one that demanded of Demonax the philosopher if philosophers did use to eat sweet cakes, Demonax made this answer, Dost thou think that bees gather their honey for fools only?

Cicero
Sherry, Puttenham

Dissolutio (Asyndeton)

also known as *continuatio, celeritas, inconjunctum, dialyton, articulus* (not to be confused with *brachylogia*) and *membrum* (not to be confused with *colon*)

Quintilian (IX, iii, 50)

Scheme. The absence of connecting particles. This figure is useful when we are speaking with special vigour: for it at once impresses the details on the mind and makes them seem more numerous than they really are. We apply this figure not merely to single words but to whole sentences . . . also known as *brachylogia* (see under ARTICULUS).

Susenbrotus (37)
Scheme. A form of *eclipsis*, in which two or more words, phrases or clauses are joined, not by conjunctions but by commas inserted in their place.

Hoskins (38)
Where substantive to substantive or word to word are joined ... where many *ands* are spared. . . . It fits well the even phrases and interpretations of an eloquent tongue that seems ... to contain many parts ... which stick in the hearer's senses.

EXAMPLES

Wilson (205)
Obey the king, fear his laws, keep thy vocation, do right, seek rest, like well a little, use all men, as thou wouldst they should use thee.

Hoskins (38)
Her skull with beauty, her head with wisdom, her eyes with majesty, her countenance with gracefulness, her lips with lovingness.

Ad Herennium, Cicero
Trapezuntius, Erasmus, Melancthon, Sherry, Scaliger, Puttenham, Day, Peacham

Distinctio (Paradiastole)
(not to be confused with *conciliatio* also known as *paradiastole*)

Quintilian (IX, iii, 64)
Scheme. By which we distinguish between similar things, as in 'brave instead of rash'.

Hoskins (42f)
If there by any doubt or ambiguity in the words, it is better left out than distinguished; but if you are to answer any former speeches, you may disperse all clouds and remove all scruples with *distinction*. . . . Distinction of ambiguity in *matter* is a determination of the truth of general propositions, to tell wherein they are certain and wherein they are not.

EXAMPLES

Hoskins (42f)
If by *light* you mean *clear*, I am glad you do see my reasons; if by *light*
you mean *of no weight* I am sorry you do not feel them.
Travel in foreign countries settleth a young man's humours. If it be taken as
'It will enforce him to wariness and secrecy' . . . it is very profitable. . . .
But if you intend that by travelling all vanities should be taken away,
it seems not so likely and admittable; because he shall walk through
many ill examples and great liberty.

Distributio (Merismos)

also known as *digestio, diaresis, anadosis, divisio* (not to be confused with
dilemma or *dialysis*) and *enumeratio* (not to be confused with the other
enumeratio)

Cicero (*De Oratore*, III, liii, 203)
Scheme. Our statement may be distributed into parts.

Wilson (185f)
Scheme. When we apply to everybody such things as are due to them,
declaring every one in his vocation. . . . When we divide the whole
into several parts . . . comprehending our whole talk within the compass of the same.

Scaliger (III, lxx)
A method of ornamentation which always enlarges the speech. It
resumes but does not repeat the initial proposition and makes an acute
or enthusiastic examination of it by parts.

Peacham (123)
Distributio is a general word comprehending diverse special kinds by
which we dilate and spread abroad the general kind . . . *divisio, partitio,
enumeratio.*

Scheme. *Divisio* . . . divideth the general kind into special kinds, yet
not in a dialectical form but in a rhetorical manner for amplification's
sake.

EXAMPLES

Wilson (185f)
It is the duty of a king to have an especial care over his whole realm.
It is the office of his nobles, to cause the king's will to be fulfilled, and
with all diligence to further his laws, and to see justice done everywhere.
It is the part of a subject, faithfully to do his prince's commandment,
and with a willing heart to serve him at all needs.

Peacham (123)
Ask the cattle and they shall inform thee, the fowls of the air and they
shall tell thee, the increase of the earth and it shall show thee, or the
fishes of the sea and they shall certify thee.

Hoskins (23)
He apparelleth himself with great distinction. For the stuff, his clothes
were more rich than glittering; as for the fashion, rather usual for his
sort than fantastical for his invention; for colour, more grave and
uniform than wild and light; for fitness, made as well for ease of exercise as to set forth to the eye those parts which in him had most ex-
cellency.

Ad Herennium, Rutilius Lupus, Quintilian
Melancthon, Susenbrotus, Sherry, Puttenham, Day

Divisio (Dialysis)
also known as *dilemma*

Ad Herennium (IV, 52)
Scheme. This figure separates the alternatives of a question and re-
solves each by means of a reason subjoined. . . . Here the division at
once unfolds itself, briefly adding the reasons for the two or more parts.

Peacham (127)
Scheme. This figure removeth one thing from another and endeth
them both by showing a reason.
Hoskins (46)
Proposeth two sides and overthrows both.

EXAMPLES

Peacham (127)
Why should I now lay anything to thy charge, if thou beest good, thou hast not deserved it, but if thou beest naught, thou carest not for it. If I have evil spoken, bear witness of the evil: but if I have well spoken, why smitest thou me?

Hoskins (46)
You must have both ability and will to write well, for to say I can not is childish, and to say I will not is womanish.

Cicero, Rutilius Lupus, Quintilian, Rufianianus
Susenbrotus, Scaliger, Puttenham, Day

Dubitatio (Aporia)
also known as *addubitatio, deliberatio, diaporesis*

Quintilian (IX, ii, 19)
Scheme. *Dubitatio* may lend an impression of truth to our statements when, for example, we pretend to be at a loss where to begin or end, or to decide what particularly requires to be said or not said ... we may equally pretend that we had felt hesitation on the subject.

Susenbrotus (63)
Scheme. When we hesitate in perplexity over which to choose of two or more alternatives. These alternatives may relate to our matter or the means of expressing it.

Peacham (109)
Scheme. The speaker showeth that he doubteth either where to begin for the multitude of matters or what to do or say in some strange and doubtful thing. . . . Sometimes he doubteth what word to use.

EXAMPLES

Fraunce (95)
But, alas, sure I am not, that *Cleophilia* is such as can answer my love: and if she be, how can I think she will? since this disguising must needs

82

come for some forsaken conceit. And either way, wretched *Gynecia*, where canst thou find any small ground-plot for hope to dwell upon?

Peacham (109)
Of what shall I first complain o judges? or where shall I first begin? Of what or whom shall I call for help, of the immortal gods, or of the Roman people? or shall I most pitifully crave your defence who have the highest authority?
Whether he took them from his fellows more impudently, gave them to an harlot more lasciviously, removed them from the Roman people more wickedly or altered them more presumptuously, I cannot well declare.

Hoskins (48)
Whom shall I blame? What shall I pretend? Shall I make learning hateful to you by my reprehensions? Shall I make my silence accessory to your idleness?

Ad Herennium, Cicero, Rutilius Lupus, Aquila, Fortunatianus
Melancthon, Talaeus, Wilson, Puttenham, Day

Effictio (Prosographia)
(not to be confused with *conformatio* also known as *prosographia*) also known as *prosopographia*

Ad Herennium (IV, 63)
When the corporeal appearance or form of any being is represented or depicted in words clearly enough to be recognised.

Erasmus (53)
The description of personal appearance.

Puttenham (238f)
Scheme. Describes as true or natural or feigns as artificial or not true . . . the visage, speech and countenance of any person absent or dead.

Peacham (135)
Scheme. By which the very person of a man as of a feigned, is by his form, stature, manners, studies, doings, affections . . . so described

that it may appear a plain and lively picture painted in tables and set
before the eyes of the hearer.

EXAMPLES

Peacham (135)

We may by the circumstances of age describe an old man . . . with
crooked limbs, and trembling joints, his head white, his eyes hollow,
his sight dim, his hearing thick, his hands shaking, his legs bowing, his
colour pale, his skin wrinkled, weak of memory, childish yet covetous,
suspicious, testy, greedy of news, credulous, misliking of the present
world and praising of former times.

Susenbrotus, Sherry, Scaliger

Elevatio (Diasyrmos)

also known as *irrisio, vexatio*

Fortunatianus (101)

With this amusing device we refute what has been said by our adversaries.

Susenbrotus (16)

Trope. A form of mockery by which we deny and refute what has
been said by our adversary.

Peacham (39f)

Trope. By which the arguments of an adversary are either depraved
or rejected . . . by some base similitude or ridiculous example to which
the adversary's objection or argument is compared. . . . In grave dis-
putations it is unseemly.

EXAMPLES

Peacham (39)

Cicero for Murena against Cato speaketh much in this manner, and
also against Sulpitius disputing in the civil law.

Aquila, Rufinianus
Sherry, Scaliger

Enumeratio

Ad Herennium (II, 47)
Part of the conclusion of an oration. When we gather together and recall the points we have made—briefly, that the speech may not be repeated in entirety, but that the memory of it may be refreshed; and we shall reproduce all the points in order.

Peacham (125f)
Scheme. The third species under *distributio*. When the subject is divided into accidents, the matter into antecedents, the effect into causes, and into things annexed and following after the effect. . . . Also by this figure the orator distributeth to particular persons their particular duties.

EXAMPLES

Peacham (125)
What may we think of man when we consider the heavy burden of his misery, the weakness of his patience, the imperfection of his understanding, the conflicts of his counsels, the insatiety of his mind, the brevity of his life and the certainty of his death?

Peacham (126)
Antony was the cause of civil war, of three slain armies of Roman people, of the death of many noble citizens, of overthrowing the authority of the senate, and finally of all evils whatsoever.

Veltkirchius, Sherry

Error

Cicero (*De Oratore*, III, liii, 205)
Scheme. We may introduce topics to lead our hearers into error.

Wilson (188)
Scheme. When we think much otherwise than the truth is.

Scaliger (III, xcii)
Under *ironia*. This figure was invented by Cicero. It can be brought about by figurative means, or through the arrangement of a whole passage.

EXAMPLES

Wilson (188)
When we have conceived a good opinion of some one man, and are often deceived, to say, 'Who would have thought that he ever would have done so. Now of all men on earth I would have least suspected him. But such is the world.'
You think such a man a worthy personage, and of much honesty, but I will prove that he is much otherwise: a man would not think it, but if I do not prove it, I will give you my head.

Evasio

Scaliger (III, xlv)
Under *tractatio*. When we merely touch upon a matter and then forsake it.

EXAMPLE

Scaliger (III, xlv)
By which duty of thine?

Exaggeratio

Scaliger (III, xlvi)
Under *tractatio*. Like *hyperbole*, the exaggerated word is used in order to stir the following emotions in the audience: praise, envy, indignation. It is used mainly in the full style.

EXAMPLES

Scaliger (III, xlvi)

Alas by what fates was the hero tossed, of what long sufferings in wars did he sing.

My fleet lost, I saved my companions from death.

Excitatio (Egersis)

Scaliger (III, lxi)

Under *tractatio*. When we arouse the audience from some languid state of consciousness or from a feeling of boredom. We may use an *acclamatio* (a brief rousing ending), an invocation, a digression which affirms or denies or prohibits something, or we may admonish the audience not to sleep.

EXAMPLES

Scaliger (III, lxi)

Now lay open Helicon, goddesses!

Flee swiftly shepherd, flee the hostile roars!

Exclamatio (Ecphonesis)

Cicero (*Orator*, xxxix, 135)

Scheme. We may utter exclamations of admiration or grief.

Quintilian (IX, ii, 27)

Scheme. When such exclamations are genuine, they are not schemes . . . it is only those which are simulated and artfully designed which can with any certainty be regarded as schemes.

G   87

Susenbrotus (61ff)
Scheme. An expression of grief or indignation on behalf of men, cities, places, times or things. . . . It is unreasonable to use this figure when dealing with things of little emotional significance.

Fraunce (63ff)
Scheme. Exclamation is expressed by some note of exclamation, either put down, or understood: an excellent instrument to stir up diverse affections, sometimes wonder and imagination . . . despair . . . wishing . . . indignation . . . derision.

Hoskins (33)
Exclamation is not lawful but in extremity of motion.

EXAMPLES

Fraunce (71)

> O fauns, o fairies all, and do you see
> And suffer such a wrong? a wrong I know
> That *Nico* must with *Pas* compared be.

Fraunce (72)
O miserable wretch, whither do thy destinies guide thee?

Peacham (62)
O how amiable are thy tabernacles thou Lord of hosts?
O most wicked presumption, from whence art thou sprung up to cover the earth with falsehood and deceit?

Hoskins (33)
O tyrant heaven, traitor earth, blind providence, no justice! How is this done! How is this suffered? Hath this world a government?

Hoskins (34)
O sun! O you heavens, deserts! O virtue! O imperfect proportion!

Ad Herennium
Melancthon, Talaeus, Sherry, Wilson, Scaliger, Puttenham, Day

Exclusio

Scaliger (III, lxi)
If we want to dismiss a point in favour of our opponents rather than a point against us; that sort of dismissal has been called *exclusio*.

EXAMPLE
Scaliger (III, lxi)
No more could Drances atone for this by his death if this is the anger of the Gods, nor if it is courage and glory could he remove it.

Execratio (Ara)

also known as *imprecatio*

Cicero (*De Oratore*, III, liii, 205)
Scheme. Execrations.

Scaliger (III, lxix)
Under *tractatio*. This figure is used, often with *rejectio*, to say things which are abhorrent and which cannot be proved.

Peacham (64)
Scheme. A form of speech by which the orator detesteth and curseth some person or thing for the evils which they bring with them or for the wickedness which is in them.

EXAMPLES
Peacham (64)
O most abominable impiety, worthy to be buried in the bottom of the earth.
Woe to the bloodthirsty city which is full of lies and robbery.
Let the ungodly have domination over him and let Satan stand at his right hand, when sentence is given upon him, let him be condemned, and let his prayer be turned to sin, let his days be few.

89

Rufinianus

Melancthon, Talaeus (Melancthon and Talaeus both have this as a sub-species under exclamatio)*, Sherry*

Exemplum (Paradigma)
also known as *propositio*

Ad Herennium (IV, 62)

When we cite something done or said in the past, along with the definite naming of the doer or utterer. . . . It renders a thought more brilliant when used for no other purpose than beauty; clearer, when throwing more light upon what was somewhat obscure; more plausible when giving the thought greater verisimilitude; more vivid when expressing the matter so lucidly it can almost be touched with the hand.

Erasmus (76ff)

For plenitude of matter. A form of rhetorical proof. We relate the deeds of particular men, either historical or fabulous. *Exemplum* may be employed inductively to convince the audience that we speak the truth.

Wilson (190f)

Scheme. To persuade. . . . Much are they to be commended, which search chronicles of all ages, and compare the state of our elders with this present time. . . . Unequal examples commend much the matter . . . when the weaker is brought in against the stronger.

Peacham (186ff)

Scheme. The rehearsal of a deed or a saying past applying it to our purpose whereof there be two kinds, the one true which is taken from chronicles and histories of credit and is of great force to move, persuade and inflame men with the love of virtue. . . . The other kind of example is feigned by poets and inventors of fables for delectations sake . . . the use whereof ought to be very rare, namely in great and grave causes.

EXAMPLES

Wilson (190)

If children be faithful, much more ought men to be faithful.

Wilson (191)
Doves seeing a hawk gather all together, teaching us none other thing, but in adversity to stick one to another.

Wilson (196)
We read of Danae the fair damsel, whom Jupiter tempted full oft, and could never have his pleasure, till at length he made it rain gold, and so as she sat in her chimney, a great deal fell upon her lap, the which she took gladly and kept it there, within the which gold Jupiter himself was comprehended, whereby is none other thing else signified, but that women have been, and will be overcome with money.

Peacham (187)
If they were kings how they ruled and governed, if patriarchs, how they lived, if wise men what they said, if fools, what they committed, if godly what they respected.

Peacham (188)
Feigned examples . . . from poet's inventions, and from the devices of apologies and fables attributed to brute creatures, as to beasts, birds, fishes, bees, ants and creeping worms, also to trees, herbs, fountains, meadows, mountains and valleys, in like manner to the sun, moon and stars.

Cicero, Quintiliam, Rufinianus, Fortunatianus
Melancthon, Susenbrotus, Sherry, Scaliger, Puttenham, Day

Expeditio
also known as *enumeratio* (not to be confused with the other *enumeratio* of which *expeditio* is a species)

Ad Herennium (IV, 40)
When we list the several ways by which something could have been brought about and, dismissing the rest, leave one upon which we insist.

Puttenham (233)
Scheme. By a manner of speech both figurative and argumentative . . .
we do briefly set down all our best reasons . . . and reject them all saving
one.

Hoskins (45)
Reckoning upon diverse parts, destroys all but the one you mean to
rest upon. . . . This enumeration and inference thereupon, is that which
the logicians call induction.

EXAMPLE

Hoskins (45)
One of these courses must be taken: either you must diligently observe
or practise these rules or deny that ever you received instructions, or
allege want of capacity in yourself or want of use of them in your life.
That they are unnecessary you cannot say. . . . That you are uncapable
is a slander and contradiction to your own conscience and my experience. . . . And to say you had never any directions were to give
your two eyes the lie. . . . Therefore must your labour conspire with
my inventions, and so must you unexcusably become skilful.

Melancthon, Susenbrotus, Sherry, Day, Peacham

Experientia (Apodixis)
also known as *authentica*

Peacham (86f)
Scheme. The orator groundeth his saying upon general and common
experience. It differeth from *martyria* in this, that in *martyria* the orator
confirmeth his saying by the testimony of his own experience, in this
he inferreth his reason and confirmation from known principles which
experience doth prove and no man can deny. . . . To this place do belong
many proverbs and common sayings which are taken from general
proof and experience.

EXAMPLES

Peacham (86f)

Whatever a man soweth that shall he also reap.

They that go down to the sea in ships, and occupy their business in the great waters, they see the works of the Lord, and his wonders in the deep.

Trust not a horse's heel nor a dog's tooth.

Cicero, Quintilian

Expolitio (Exergasia)

Ad Herennium (IV, 54f)

When we dwell on the same topic and yet seem to say something ever new. It is accomplished in two ways: by merely repeating the same idea, or by descanting upon it. We shall not repeat the same thing precisely. . . . Our changes will be of three kinds: in the words, the delivery and the treatment. . . . The third kind of change, in the treatment, will occur if we transform the thought into the form of dialogue or *exuscitatio*.

Erasmus (83)

For plenitude of matter. A device whereby we dwell a long time on the same point, varying the same *sententia* in different ways.

Susenbrotus (90)

Scheme. *Expolitio* or ornamentation by varying the words is *interpretatio* or *synonymia*. *Expolitio* through discussing other matters . . . may be seen as a form of argument . . . a polished proof or the explication of an argument.

Puttenham (247)

The last and principle figure of our poetical ornament . . . to polish our speech . . . and attire it with copious and pleasant amplifications and much variety of sentence all running upon one point and to one intent.

Peacham (196)
In using exposition it is very necessary to avoid *Tautologies*.

EXAMPLES

Peacham (194)
Sextus Roscius is convicted that he slew his father. Did Sextus Roscius slay his father?
The country chiding with Cataline. . . . 'There hath no abominable or wicked deed been heard or seen these many years but through thee: no naughty facts without thee: thou only hast slain many citizens, and never yet punished: thou hast vexed and robbed thy fellows, and nothing said unto thee: thou hast not only been able to neglect laws and statutes, but also to overthrow them and break them in pieces.'

Cicero
Melancthon, Sherry

Exprobatio (Onedismos)

Robortellus (49)
When something is neatly criticised and derided by exposing to attack things in it that are disgusting.

Peacham (73f)
Scheme. The speaker upbraideth his adversary of ingratitude and impiety . . . most specially to reprove and rebuke ingratitude.

EXAMPLES

Peacham (74)
    No goddess never was thy dam, nor thou of Dardans kind,
    Thou traitor wretch but under rocks and mountains rough unkind
    Thou wert begot, some brood thou art of Beast or Monster wild,
    Some Tigers thee did nurse and gave to thee their milk unmild.
The prophet *Esay* . . . in a similitude of a vineyard fruitfully planted and carefully fenced doth set before the peoples' eyes God's goodness, . . . and by the wild and evil fruit which that vineyard brought forth, he accuseth them of most sinful ingratitude.

Extenuatio (Meiosis) ✓
also known as *minutio, detractio, diminutio*

Quintilian (VIII, iii, 50)
Meagreness and inadequacy of expression. . . . But *meiosis* may be deliberately employed and is then a scheme.

Quintilian (VIII, iv, 28)
Diminution may be effected by the same method as amplification [see under AMPLIFICATIO].

Erasmus (35)
For plenitude of words. Sometimes it has the savour of *hyperbole* as in 'shorter than a pigmy'.

Scaliger (III, lxxxi)
Under *eclipsis*. It may be simple or complex. We may detract from the value of something by substituting a worse name for the name of something known already to be bad, or by using a lesser style to phrase a particular proposition. . . . When it is complex, this figure resembles a comparison. . . . True *extenuatio* is a form of criticism, not mere understatement.

Hoskins (35f)
Descends by the same steps that amplification ascends by . . . two ways of diminishing by single terms; one, by denying the contrary. . . . The second way is by denying the right use of the word but by error of some, . . . the former . . . sometimes in ironious sort goes for amplification.

EXAMPLES
Wilson (181)
To say, that the one had his leg pricked with a sword, when perchance he had a great wound.

Peacham (168)
To call a learned doctor a pretty scholar, . . . a raging railer a testy fellow.

Hoskins (35)
Not the wisest man that I ever saw (for *a man of small wisdom*).
Those fantastical-minded people which children and musicians call lovers.
This colour of mine, which she in the deceivable style of affection would entitle beautiful.

Hoskins (36)
No mean man (for *a great personage*).

Ad Herennium
Melancthon, Susenbrotus, Sherry, Puttenham, Day

Exuscitatio

Ad Herennium (IV, 55)
When we are seen to be moved by what we are saying and thus we stir the emotions of the audience with us.

Susenbrotus (99)
Scheme. When the audience sees the speaker to be emotionally moved and is moved with him . . . a form of *expolitio*.

Peacham (177)
Scheme. When the speaker being much moved with some vehement affection in himself doth show it by the utterance of his speech and thereby moveth the minds of his hearers, and is used . . . for great praises or dispraises.

EXAMPLES

Peacham (177)
What man is he, be he never so envious, never so malicious, never so ambitious of honour, but must needs commend this man. . . .
Who is of so careless a mind, that seeing these things can hold his peace and let them pass? You put my father to death before he was condemned, and being so put to death you registered him among con-

demned men, you thrust me out of mine own house by violence, you possessed my patrimony, what will you more?

Day

Fabella (Apologia)

Erasmus (84f)
For plenitude of matter. Near to the class of the fabulous . . . to give greater pleasure by a certain witty imitation of customs . . . and to place the truth before the eye of the beholder. . . . The interpretation or *epimythion* may come at the beginning or the end.

Wilson (197f)
Scheme. The feigned fables, such as are attributed unto brute beasts . . . the parts of a man's body, etc.

Scaliger (III, lxxxiv)
Under *allegory*. A fictive narrative concerning any subject, that uses personification and describes emotional or moral events. . . . It is not just the aspect of fiction that corresponds to debates in philosophy . . . but has wider uses, and one can describe as *apologos* the writing in which a primary and essential significance is perceived in different ideas.

Hoskins (10)
A similitude acted by fiction in beasts.

EXAMPLES

Wilson (198)
The Roman Menenius Agrippa, alleging upon a time, a fable of the conflict made betwixt the parts of a man's body, and his belly.
For when many flies stood feeding upon his raw flesh and had well fed themselves, he was contented at another's persuasion, to have them flapped away: whereupon there ensued such hungry flies afterwards, that the sorry fox being all alone, was eaten up almost to the hard bone, and therefore cursed the time that he ever agreed to any such evil counsel. In like manner if you will change officers . . . whereas now you

live being but only bitten . . . because they are filled and have enough, that heretofore sucked so much of your blood.

Hoskins (10)
There was a lamb in a castle and an elephant and a fox besieged it. The elephant would have assailed the castle, but he would not swim over the river. The fox would make a hole in the earth to get under it, but he feared the river would have sunk in upon him and drowned him.

Melancthon

Fabula (Mythos)

Erasmus (70f)
For plentitude of matter. It is beyond question that in the skilful authors of antiquity, in all the creations of the ancient poets, allegory is found. . . . These fictions are effective because they have been devised by those whose authority has the force of precept. They also have force as *exempla*.

Scaliger (III, lxxxiv)
Under *allegory*. A fictional narration to represent the truth by presenting images of the truth: feigned speeches which could have been true or invented, definitions of things, countries or substances. The subjects of myth include the gods, the sun, the moon, the sea, and the earth. The hieroglyphs are related to myth.

Hoskins (10)
A form of similitude . . . a *poet's tale*, acted for the most part, by gods and men.

EXAMPLES

Hoskins (10)
Let Spenser tell you a tale of a Faery Queen, and Ovid of Diana, then it is a poet's tale.

Rutilius Lupus, Aquila

Familiaritas (Syntomia)

Cicero (Orator, xi, 139)
Scheme. When we address our audience in terms of intimacy or familiarity.

Veltkirchius (143f)
Scheme. A brief, direct and plain way of speaking, by which things are dealt with briefly and explained clearly in few words. The topics treated are not lingered over.

EXAMPLES
Veltkirchius (143)
This manner of speaking is found in Aristotle, Sallust, Emilius, Probus, Justinus and Terence.

Quintilian

Figura (Schema)

Quintilian (IX, i, 1ff)
Generic term for a class of rhetorical devices. They add force and charm to our matter . . . when we give our language a conformation other than the obvious and ordinary. . . . In the special rhetorical sense *figura* or *schema* means a rational change in meaning or language from the ordinary and simple form. . . . There are two classes of scheme, schemes of thought (*dianoias*), that is, of the mind, feeling or concepts, and figures of words (*lexeos*), of diction, expression, language or style.

Fraunce (26)
A figure is a certain decking of speech, whereby the usual and simple fashion thereof is altered and changed to that which is more elegant and conceited. For as a trope is of single words, so a figure of coupled and conjoined. . . . A figure is either in the word or in the sentence. A figure of the word is that whereby the words do sweetly and fitly sound among themselves.

99

Fraunce (63)
The figures in sentences in the whole sentence express some motion of the mind. These are more forcible and apt to persuade.

Peacham (1577, Ci)
A form of words, oration or sentence made new by art and differing from the vulgar manner and custom of writing or speaking.

Ad Herennium, Cicero, Rutilius Lupus, Aquila, Rufinianus
Trapezuntius, Melancthon, Erasmus, Susenbrotus, Talaeus, Scaliger, Sherry, Wilson, Puttenham, Hoskins

Figura (Typos)
also known as *modellum*

Scaliger (III, xxxiii)
Under *tractatio*. *Typos* signifies a configuration or formula which is like an architect's model of the structure of the whole.... From the lineaments and dimensions of this model we may deduce the proportion of the whole work.

Flexus (Peribole)

Veltkirchius (38)
Scheme. This is an involuted and prolix form of speech, ... one species of which is *irmos* [see under SERIES].... A typical form of *flexus* is the circumlocutory historical speech.

EXAMPLES
Veltkirchius (38)
Many examples found in historians; Livy, Sallust and Caesar.

Frequentatio

Ad Herennium (IV, 52)
When points dispersed throughout the argument are brought together in one place. The effect is to make the speech more impressive, more bitter, or more accusatory.

Scaliger (III, xlii)
Under *tractatio*. Multiple repetition, too much of which causes annoyance.

Peacham (151)
Scheme. A figure by which matter being dispersed throughout the whole oration is gathered together into one place, whereby the oration is made more pithy and sharp, or thus: when many arguments being scattered here and there one from another are gathered together ... and laid before the eyes of the hearer.

EXAMPLES

Peacham (151)
When all is done what vice is he free from, what is the cause Judges why you would deliver him? He is a betrayer of his own chastity, he lieth in wait to do mischief, he is covetous, intemperate, vicious, proud, wicked to his parents, unkind to his friends, troublesome to his kin.
Now truly the fortune of the Roman people seemeth to me both hard and cruel, which had seen and suffered these men many years to vaunt against the commonwealth: they had with idolatory and adultery profaned and polluted the most holy religions, they broke in pieces the most substantial decrees of the Senate, they ransomed themselves with bribes before the judges, ... they cut in sunder the records of all orders made for the safety of the commonwealth.

Melancthon, Sherry

Gradatio (Climax)
also known as *concatenatio*

Quintilian (IX, iii, 54f)
Scheme. A more obvious and less natural application of art [than *acervatio*] and should therefore be more sparingly employed. It ... repeats what has already been said and, before passing to a new point, dwells on those which precede.

Scaliger (IV, xxxi)
Scheme. The ladder form, whereby the same word repeated links the step preceding to the one following.

Fraunce (38)
Scheme. A reduplication continued by divers degrees and steps . . . of the same word or sound, for these two be of one kind.

Hoskins (12f)
A kind of *anadiplosis* [see under REDUPLICATIO] leading by degrees and making the last word a step to the further meaning. If it be turned to an argument, it is a *sorites* . . . or climbing argument, joining the first and the last with an *ergo*. . . . This in penned speech is too academical, but in discourse more passable and plausible. . . . This figure hath his time when you are well entered into discourse and have procured attention and mean to rise and amplify.

EXAMPLES

Puttenham (208)
> Peace makes plenty, plenty makes pride,
> Pride breeds quarrel, and quarrel brings war.

Fraunce (39)
> Loving in truth, and fain in verse my love to show,
> That the dear she might take some pleasure of my pain,
> Pleasure might cause her read, reading might make her know
> Knowledge might pity win, and pity grace obtain.

Hoskins (12f)
You could not enjoy your goodness without government, nor government without a magistrate, nor magistrate without obedience, and no obedience where every one upon his private passion doth interpret the doings of the rulers . . . (to make it a *sorites* you add an *ergo*, you cannot enjoy your own goods where every man upon his private passion etc.).

Cicero, Aquila, Rufinianus
Melancthon, Susenbrotus, Talaeus, Sherry, Wilson, Day, Peacham

Gratiarium actio (Eucharistia)

Peacham (101f)
Scheme. The speaker giveth thanks for benefits received . . . used with much acknowledging of the benefits received, and the unworthiness of the receiver . . . or with a confession of the unableness of the receiver to requite the giver.

EXAMPLES

Peacham (101)
To thee O Caesar we give most hearty thanks, yea great thanks we yield to thee.

Peacham (102)
I am not worthy of the least of all thy mercies, and all the truth which thou hast showed unto thy servant, for with my staff came I over this Jordan, and now I have two droves.
What shall I give unto the Lord for all the benefits towards me? or for all the benefits he hast bestowed upon me.

Heratio (Palilogia)
also known as *duplicatio, diaphora, ploche* (not to be confused with *copulatio*)

Susenbrotus (52)
Scheme. When the same word is repeated emphasising by the repetition a particular aspect of its meaning.

Scaliger (IV, xxix)
Scheme. Not merely repetition of the same sound, but repetition of the word as a unit of meaning. The meaning is inevitably altered on the second appearance of the word.

Peacham (44)
Scheme. *Ploche,* a proper name being repeated signifieth another thing.
. . . May signify the constant nature and permanent quality of a man well known, by the repetition of his name.

H   103

Peacham (45)
Scheme. *Diaphora*, like *ploche* but that repeateth a proper name, this a common word.

EXAMPLES

Peacham (44)
Yet at that day Memmius was Memmius.

Peacham (45)
What man is there living but will pity such a case: if he be a man.

Rutilius Lupus, Aquila, Rufinianus
Melancthon

Humiliatio (Tapinosis)

Quintilian (VIII, iii, 48)
Vice of style. Meanness . . . when the grandeur or dignity of anything is diminished by the word used.

Puttenham (185)
Scheme. If ye abase your thing or matter by ignorance or error in the choice of your word . . . a vicious manner of speech.

Puttenham (259)
Vice. To use such words and terms as do diminish and abase the matter . . . by impairing the dignity, height, vigour or majesty of the cause the orator takes in hand.

Peacham (168)
Vice. Excess of *meiosis*. When the dignity or majesty of a high matter is much defaced by the baseness of a word.

EXAMPLES

Peacham (168)
To call the ocean a stream, or the Thames a brook, a foughten field a fray, great wisdom pretty wit, an oration a tale.
If one should say to a king, may it please your Mastership.

Melancthon, Veltkirchius, Susenbrotus, Sherry

Ignocentia (Syggnome)

Robortellus (45ᵛ)
Scheme. To forgive. Belongs among those figures Quintilian rejects
as *affectiones animi*, and not figures.

Peacham (98)
Scheme. The speaker, being a patient of many and great injuries, or
some one great and grievous wrong pronounceth pardon and forgiveness to his adversary, who was the worker of all his misery.

EXAMPLES

Peacham (98)
Father forgive them, for they know not what they do.
Lord, lay not this sin to their charge.
To whom ye forgive any thing, I forgive also.

Illusio (Ironia)

also known as *dissimulatio, irrisio*

Quintilian (VIII, vi, 54f)
Trope. That class of *allegory* in which the meaning is contrary to that
suggested by the words . . . this is made evident to the understanding
either by the delivery, the character of the speaker or the nature of the
subject, for if any one of these is out of keeping with the words it becomes clear that the intention of the speaker is other than what he
actually says. Under irony Quintilian places *sarcasmos, asteismos, anti-
phrasis, parimia* and *mycterismos*.

Quintilian (IX, ii, 44f)
Scheme. In both cases [scheme and trope] we understand something
the opposite of what is actually said. . . . The trope is franker in its
meaning . . . but in the schematic form of irony the speaker disguises
his entire meaning, the disguise being apparent rather than confessed.
In the trope the conflict is purely verbal: in the scheme the meaning . . .
conflicts with the language and tone of voice adopted . . . a sustained
series of tropes develops into the scheme *ironia*.

Scaliger (III, lxxxv)

A generic term covering the group of figures in which the word is contrary to the sense. This is apprehended not from the act of speaking itself, but from the nature of the speech act. It differs from allegory in that allegory points out what things have in common and brings them together, whereas irony brings together things which are contraries, pointing out the basis of their separation.

Fraunce (10)

Trope. By naming one contrary intendeth another. The special grace where of is in jesting and merry conceited speeches. This trope continued maketh a most sweet allegory, and it is perceived by the contrariety of the matter itself, or by the manner of utterance quite differing from the sense of the words.

EXAMPLES

Wilson (181)

An other, being much grieved with his folly, said 'Sir I have taken you for a plain meaning gentleman, but I now know there is not a more deceitful body in all England: . . . for I took him heretofore for a sober witty young man, but now I perceive he is a foolish babbling fellow, and therefore I am sure he hath deceived me, like a false crafty child as he is.'

Fraunce (12)

O notable affection, for love of the father, to kill the wife, and disinherit the children. O single minded modesty, to aspire to no less than the princely diadem.

Hoskins (30)

Milo had but slender strength, that carried an ox a furlong on his track and then killed him with his fist and ate him to his breakfast.
Titormus had a reasonable good arm, that could hold two bulls by the tail, the one in one hand, the other in the other, and never be stirred out of the place by their violent pulling. (Here *slender*, *reasonable* amplify as much as if you had said *great*, *exceeding*, *incredible*.)

Cicero, Aquila, Rufinianus
Melancthon, Susenbrotus, Talaeus, Sherry, Puttenham, Day, Peacham

Imaginatio (Pathopoeia)

Sherry (Eii)
Scheme. *Dionysis* or intention or imagination whereby fear, anger, madness, hatred, envy and like other perturbations of mind is showed and described, and *oictros* or commiseration whereby . . . pity is moved, or forgiveness.

Peacham (143f)
Scheme. The orator moveth the minds of his hearers to some vehemence of affection, indignation, fear, envy, hatred. . . . Two kinds . . . when the orator being moved himself with any of these affections (sorrow excepted) doth bend and apply his speech to stir his hearers to the same. . . .This kind is called Imagination to which belong *exclamatio, obtestatio, imprecatio, optatio, exuscitatio, interrogatio*. . . . The other kind is when the orator by declaring some lamentable cause, moveth his hearers to pity and compassion, to shew mercy and to pardon offences.

EXAMPLES

Peacham (144)
Examples of *imaginatio* are common in tragedies, but of mirth and laughter in comedies.
To pardon offences the perorations of Cicero are good precedents.

Rufinianus, Veltkirchius

Imago (Icon)

Ad Herennium (IV, 62)
The comparison of one form or figure or attitude with another, implying a certain resemblance between them. It may be used for praise or abuse.

Erasmus (78)
For plenitude of thought. *Imago* is not a similitude. It makes for **vivid** presentation or emphasis or enjoyment rather than proof.

Scaliger (III, l)
Under *tractatio*. Two things are understood by the intellect under one thing, by reason of their assimilation into the image of that one thing. . . . An apt device for the brief style.

Puttenham (243f)
Scheme. By portrait or imagery we liken an human person to another in countenance, stature, speech, or other quality . . . alluding to the painter's term who yieldeth to the eye a beautiful representation of the thing.

EXAMPLES

Puttenham (243)
Recommending the Queen for wisdom, beauty and magnanimity one likened her to the serpent, the lion and the angel.

Peacham (145f)
A ravenous and venomous person . . . even as a crested dragon which with burning eyes, sharp teeth, crooked claws, gaping mouth, runneth hither and thither, and looketh every where whom he may find to spit his poison upon.
The cart of covetousness is borne upon four wheels, Pusillanimity, Discourtesy, Contempt of God and Forgetfulness of death: it is drawn with two cattle in one yoke: Greedy catching, and Fast holding: to these there is one driver: Vehement desire of increasing. This driver to move speedily forward, useth two sharp whips: Greediness of getting, and Fear of losing. This vice as you see, hath but one servant, because he is loth to hire many.

Cicero, Quintilian, Rufinianus
Melancthon, Susenbrotus, Sherry, Wilson, Day

Imitatio (Mimesis)
also known as *hypocrisis* and *ethopoeia* (not to be confused with *notatio*)

Ad Herennium (I, 10)
To discredit our adversary by imitating him.

Quintilian (IX, ii, 58f)
The imitation of other person's characteristics . . . serves to excite the
gentler emotions. . . . It may be concerned either with words or deeds
. . . We may imitate our own words and deeds in a similar fashion by
relating some act or statement of our own.

Peacham (138f)
Scheme. An imitation of speech whereby the orator conterfeiteth not
only what one said but also his utterance, pronounciation and gesture,
imitating everything as it was.

EXAMPLES

Quintilian (IX, ii, 58)
I didn't see your drift, 'A little girl was stolen from this place; my
mother brought her up as her own daughter. She was known as my
sister. I want to get her away to restore her to her relations'.

Peacham (139)
Well described in Aesop's ass, unaptly imitating the fawning dog.

Rufinianus
Sherry

Importunitas

Puttenham (267)
Vice of style. Unfitness or undecency of the time.

EXAMPLE

Puttenham (267)
What a devil tellest thou to me of justice, now thou seeest me use
force and do the best I can to bereave mine enemy of his town?

Improprietas (Acyron)

Quintilian (VIII, ii, 3f)
Vice of style. While there is no special merit in the form of propriety
which consists in calling things by their real names, it is a fault to fly

to the opposite extreme . . . Every word that lacks appropriateness will not necessarily suffer from the fault of positive *improprietas* because there are many things which have no proper term.

Peacham (1577, Di)
Vice of style. An unproper speaking either in word or sense, or when a word is not used in his proper place.

Peacham (61)
Vice. To attribute unproper adjuncts to the subjects . . . an unproper speaking in form and sense.

EXAMPLES

Peacham (Di)
I fear I shall make you smart for this (not, *I hope I shall make you smart for this*).

Peacham (61)
Rich men are envied for their wisdom, and holy men for their wealth.

Sherry, Puttenham

Improvisum

Cicero (*De Oratore*, III, liv, 207)
Scheme. Introduction of the unexpected.

Quintilian (VIII, v, 15)
A type of *sententia* which depends on surprise for its effect.

EXAMPLE

Quintilian (VIII, v, 15)
When Vibius Crispus, in denouncing the man who wore a breast-plate when strolling in the forum and alleged that he did so because he feared for his life, cried 'Who gave you leave to be such a coward?'

Incisum (Comma)

also known as *articulus* (not to be confused with *brachylogia*)

Veltkirchius (36ᵛ)
Scheme. A brief verbal unit . . . used in daily and familiar talk.

Scaliger (IV, xxv)
Scheme. A phrase which does not contain a verb. Alternatively, *comma* means a part of a sentence. Each *membrum* is composed of *commata*, each period of *membra*.

EXAMPLE

Scaliger (IV, xxv)
Arma and *virumque cano* are the two *commata* of the *colon*, *Arma virumque cano*.

Cicero, Quintilian
Melancthon

Incrementum (Auxesis)

also known as *progressio*

Quintilian (VIII, iv, 3f)
The first method of *amplificatio*. This may be effected by one step or several and may be carried not merely to the highest degree but even beyond it . . . a continuous and unbroken series in which each word is stronger than the last.

Erasmus (58)
For plenitude of thought. By several steps not only is a climax reached but sometimes . . . a point beyond the climax. . . . This figure looks to something higher.

Wilson (202)
Scheme. Standeth upon contrary sentences, which answer one another.

Hoskins (26)
A kind of amplification which by steps of comparison scores every degree till it come to the top, and to make the matter seem the higher

advanced sometimes descends the lower . . . an ornament in speech to begin at the lowest, that you better aspire to the height of amplification.

EXAMPLES

Wilson (202)
Thou sleeps, he wakes; thou plays, he studies; thou art ever abroad, he is ever at home; thou never waits, he still doth his attendance; thou carest for nobody, he doth his duty to all men.

Puttenham (218)
His realm, renown, liege, liberty and life.

Peacham (169)
Neither silver, gold nor precious stones might be compared to her virtues.

Hoskins (27)
To make table-talk of a mean man's name were wrong, to run upon a nobleman's title were a great scandal, to play with a prince's name were a treason; and what shall it be to make a vanity of that name which is most terrible even to tyrants and devils, and most revered even to monarchs and angels?

Melancthon, Susenbrotus, Day

Increpatio (Epiplexis)
also known as *epitimesis*

Rufinianius (60)
When we attack or refute vehemently arguments opposed to our case.

EXAMPLE

Sherry (Dii)
Cicero against Cataline: Thinkest thou that thy counsels are not known? And that we know not what thou didst the last night? And what the night before?

Inopinatum (Paradoxon)
also known as *sustentatio*

Quintilian (IX, ii, 22f)
Scheme. The unexpected: after keeping the judges in suspense for a considerable time we add something much worse . . . or after raising expectation of a most serious sequel we may drop to something which is of a trivial character and may even imply no offence at all.

Susenbrotus (64)
Scheme. We put forward a suspicion or an opinion by denying that we could have been capable of it. . . . We use words that express wonder at this state of affairs.

Puttenham (225f)
Scheme. Our poet is carried . . . to report of a thing that is marvellous . . . and to seem to speak of it . . . with some sign of admiration.

Peacham (112)
Scheme. The orator affirmeth something to be true by saying that he would not have believed it, . . . it is so strange, so great, or so wonderful that it may appear to be incredible.

EXAMPLES

Puttenham (226)

> For what the waves could never wash away
> This proper youth has wasted in a day.

Peacham (112f)
For the which hope's sake, O king Agrippa, I am accused of the Jews, why should it be thought a thing incredible unto you: that God should raise again the dead. I also thought in myself that I ought to do many contrary things against the name of Jesus of Nazareth, which thing I did also in Jerusalem, for many of the Saints I shut up in prison having received authority of the high Priest, and when they were put to death I gave the sentence.

Rufinianus, Fortunatianus
Melancthon, Day

Insultatio

Cicero (Orator, xl, 137)
Scheme. To often deride the opponent.

Susenbrotus (63)
Scheme. When we upbraid and insult our opponent with some slander and attack him, not without derision.

Puttenham (209f)
Scheme. Another figure much like to the *sarcasmus* or bitter taunt . . . is when with proud and insolent words we do upbraid a man.

EXAMPLES

Puttenham (210)

> Hye thee, and by the wild waves and wind,
> Seek Italy and realms for thee to reign,
> If piteous gods have power amidst the main,
> On ragged rocks thy penance thou mayst find.

> Go now and give thy life unto the wind,
> Trusting unto a piece of bruckle wood,
> Four inches from thy death.

Day

Interjectio (Parembole)
also known as *parathesis, brevis interpositio*

Quintilian (VIII, ii, 15)
Scheme. The insertion of one sentence in the midst of another.

Melancthon (Epitome, 520)
For *amplificatio.* An affirmation thrust into the midst of one's plea.

Scaliger (IV, xxxviii)
Scheme. When we insert into the case itself what ought to have been brought forward after the speech.

EXAMPLE

Melancthon (520)
Venus loves speed. If you seek a consummation to your love (Love believes in action) act and you will be sure.

Interpellatio

Scaliger (III, xci)
Under *ironia*. Pertains to dissimulation or pretence.

EXAMPLE

Scaliger (III, xci)
And who was the other one who mapped out in a circle the whole habitation of men? [Perhaps the shepherd speaking does not know, but on the part of the poet himself this is a pretence].

Cicero

Interpositio (Parenthesis)
also known as *circumductio, interclusio, paremptosis*

Quintilian (IX, iii, 23)
Scheme. The interruption of the continuous flow of our language by the insertion of some remark.

Scaliger (IV, i)
Two kinds; *circunductio* which amplifies by adding before and after our subject its circumstances, genus, species etc., and *epemboly* where we enlarge our speech by discussing extra things related to our subject.

Scaliger (IV, xxxviii)
Scheme. When we insert into a speech a section containing material which is outside or alien to our subject, although it may be related to it.

Peacham (198f)
Scheme. Setteth a sentence asunder by the interposition of another . . . When a sentence is cast between the speech . . . which, although it

giveth some strength, yet being taken away, it leaveth the same speech perfect enough. . . . If they be very long they cause obscurity of the sense.

EXAMPLES

Peacham (198)
At that time all vineyards (though there were a thousand vines in one, and sold for a thousand silverlings) shall be turned into briars and thorns.

Hoskins (44)
He, swelling in their humbleness (like a bubble swollen up with a small breath, broken with a great), forgetting (or not knowing) humanity, caused their heads to be struck off.

Rutilius Lupus, Rufinianus
Melancthon, Susenbrotus, Sherry, Puttenham, Day

Interpretatio (Synonymia)
also known as *paraphrasis*

Quintilian (IX, iii, 45f)
Scheme. Words of the same meaning are grouped together . . . it serves to make the sense stronger and more obvious. . . . The same device may be applied to thoughts of similar content.

Erasmus (19f)
For plenitude of words. When we use different words to express the same thought. . . . The words may never be identical in meaning from one context to another. . . . There is no word that is not the best in some particular place.

Scaliger (III, liv)
Under *tractatio.* A passage of exposition, that adds more material or interprets the subject in other words.

Scaliger (IV, xxxii)
Scheme. When we use words which differ from the words preceding them in form or sound but which mean the same, . . . possible because

we can use many names for the same thing. This figure gives variety and is the opposite of *tautologia*.

Hoskins (47)
If a short ordinary sense be oddly expressed by . . . as many other words . . . instead of any ordinary words importing any trivial sense, to take the abstract, or some consequent, similitude, note, property, or effect, and thereby declare it.

EXAMPLES

Puttenham (214)

Is he alive
Is he as I left him queaving and quick,
And hath he not yet given up the ghost?

Peacham (149)
The highest doth not allow the gifts of the wicked, and God hath no delight in the offerings of the ungodly.
How doth the child *Ascanius*? is he yet living? doth he eat the ethereal food and lieth he not yet under the cruel shades?

Hoskins (47)
Many false oaths / Plentiful perjury.
To make a great show of himself / To make a master of himself in the island.
Seeking by courtesy to undo him / Making courtesy the outside of mischief.

Ad Herennium, Cicero, Aquila
Trapezuntius, Melancthon, Susenbrotus, Sherry, Wilson, Day

Interrogatio (Erotema)
also known as *percontatio* (not to be confused with *exetasis*)

Quintilian (IX, ii, 6f)
Scheme. A question involves a figure whenever it is employed not to get information but to emphasise our point. . . . Or we may ask what

cannot be denied, or what cannot be answered . . . or to excite pity . . . or to embarrass our opponent.

Puttenham (211)
Scheme. When we ask many questions and look for none answer, speaking indeed by interrogation which we might as well say by affirmation.

Peacham (105)
Scheme. Two kinds, the one simple and plain which is when we ask with desire to receive an answer . . . The other . . . figurative . . . when we ask not with intent or desire to receive an answer but because we would thereby make our speech more sharp and vehement.

Hoskins (33)
It is very fit for a speech to many and indiscreet hearers.

EXAMPLE

Peacham (105)
The Mariners of Jonas: Tell us for whose cause are we thus troubled? What is thine occupation?
Love: How fair are thou? And how pleasant art thou, O my love? O how sweet are thy words unto my throat?

Hoskins (33)
Pirocles' oration to the seditious multitude: Did the sun ever bring fruitful harvest, but was more hot than pleasant? Have you any of your children that be not sometimes cumbersome? Have you any fathers that be not sometimes wearish? Shall we therefore curse the sun, hate our children, or disobey our parents?

Ad Herennium, Cicero, Aquila, Fortunatianus
Melancthon, Susenbrotus, Sherry, Wilson, Scaliger, Day

Interruptio (Paraposiopesis)

Scaliger (III, lxxvii)
Under *eclipsis*. When we interrupt the oration, usually with an apostrophe or exclamation of emotion, and cannot continue what we were

previously saying. A device of the grand or high style. The hearer is left in uncertainty.

EXAMPLES

Scaliger (III, lxxvii)
O blessed are they whose walls are already rising and whose rest from toil is secured!

Cicero

Inter se pugnantia

Peacham (163)
Scheme. The orator reproveth his adversary or some other person of manifest unconstancy, open hypocrisy, or insolent arrogancy.

EXAMPLES

Peacham (163)
Thou that preachest a man should not steal, yet thou stealest: thou that saist that a man should not commit adultery, yet thou breakest wedlock.
Out of one mouth proceedeth blessing and cursing, my brethren these things ought not so to be: doth a fountain send forth at one place sweet water and bitter?

Intimitatio (Noema)

Quintilian (VIII, v, 12)
Noema is employed by modern rhetoricians in the special sense of things which the speaker wishes to be understood though they are not actually said.

Erasmus (82)
For plenitude of matter. What is understood rather than expressed.

I   119

Puttenham (230)

Scheme. The obscurity of the sense lieth not in a single word but in an entire speech, whereof we do not so easily conceive the meaning but . . . by conjecture because it is witty and subtle or dark.

Hoskins (25f)

A way of amplifying that leaves the collection of greatness to our understanding, by expressing some mark of it. It exceedeth speech in silence, and makes our meaning more palpable by a touch than by a direct handling.

EXAMPLES

Wilson (180)

Ye may boldly speak for fish eating, for my master your father, hath many a time and oft, wiped his nose upon his sleeve (meaning that his father was a fishmonger).

Peacham (180)

He was never made friends with his mother and his sister: meaning that there was never any debate or contention between them.

Peacham (181)

Quintilian (VIII, v) bringeth in an example of a certain woman, who . . . cut off her brother's thumb . . . 'O brother (saith she) thou are well worthy of a perfect hand without maim' (meaning . . . that such a one should meet his own destruction, that did so oft seek it with his own will).

Hoskins (26)

He draws his sword oftener than he draws his purse.

Cicero

Melancthon, Susenbrotus, Scaliger

Inversio (Allegoria)

also known as *permutatio* (not to be confused with *enallage*)

Ad Herennium (IV, 46)

A speech which displays a meaning which is other than the letter of the words. . . . It is operated by similitude when a number of metaphors

originating in a similarity in the mode of expression are set together
. . . operates by argument when a similitude is drawn from a person,
place or thing in order to magnify or diminish. . . . It operates by contrast when, for example, a gross and prodigal man is described as
frugal and thrifty.

Quintilian (VIII, vi, 44ff)
Trope. If either presents one thing in words and another in meaning,
or else something absolutely opposed to the meaning of the words.
The first is generally produced by a series of metaphors. . . . Also
allegory without metaphor occurs where, with the exception of a
pseudonymous proper name, the words bear no more than their literal
meaning. . . . The most ornamental effect is produced by the artistic ad-
mixture of similitude, metaphor and allegory.

Erasmus (30)
For plenitude of words. Nothing but a continuous metaphor.

Erasmus (70)
It is beyond question that in the skilful authors of antiquity, in all the
creations of the ancient poets, allegory is found.

Wilson (176)
Trope. A metaphor used throughout a whole sentence, or oration. . . .
The English proverbs . . . commonly are nothing else but allegories, and
dark devised sentences.

Scaliger (III, xxxii)
The generic term for that group of figures which signify some thing
other than the words of which they are composed appear to signify.

Talaeus (5ff)
Trope. Continued *hyperbole*. It must end in the same kind of terms as
it began or else the effect is frightful . . . continued *metonymia* is also
allegory.

Fraunce (3f)
Trope. One trope continued in many, as that with what thing it began,
with the same it also end.

Puttenham (186ff)
The courtly figure . . . when we speak one thing and think another and that our words and our meanings meet not . . . no man can pleasantly utter and persuade without it, . . . the chief ringleader and captain of all other figures either in the poetical or oratory science. . . . The full allegory should not be discovered but left at large to the readers judgment and conjecture.

EXAMPLES

Peacham (26)
(By 'ship', Horace understandeth Sextus Pompeius . . . troubling the sea with a naval war)
   O ship shall new clouds carry thee again into the sea?
   What dost thou now? Strive manfully to keep the port alway.
Whose fan is in his hand, and he shall purge his floor, and gather his wheat into his barn, but will burn his chaff with unquenchable fire.

Hoskins (9)
But when that wish had once his ensign in his mind, then followed whole squadrons of longing, that so it might be a main battle of mislikings and repinings against their creation.

Cicero
Melancthon, Susenbrotus, Sherry, Day

Inversio (Epistrophe)
(not to be confused with *conversio*)

Scaliger (IV, xxxiii)
Scheme. This figure does not merely exchange the positions of two constituent parts or syllables but functions by corrupting the whole form of a word.

EXAMPLE

Scaliger (IV, xxxiii)
Chrysalo Crucisalsum.

Invitio (Ennoia)

Scaliger (III, lxxx)
Under *eclipsis*. This is a holding back of information, but it does not leave it out altogether. By a circuitous kind of statement it leads to fuller understanding.

EXAMPLE
Scaliger (III, lxxx)
Might not I have lived from wedlock free, a life without a stain, happy as beasts are happy? [This life is nevertheless a life of beasts.]

Iracundia

Cicero (*De Oratore*, III, liii, 205)
Scheme. Expressions of anger.

Wilson (200)
Scheme. When we will take the matter as hot as a toast.

EXAMPLE
Wilson (200)
We need no examples for this matter, hot men have too many, of whom they may be bold and spare not that find themselves a cold.

Quintilian

Irrisio (Sarcasmos)

Quintilian (VIII, vi, 57)
Trope. A kind of allegory, to disguise bitter taunts in gentle words by way of wit.

Susenbrotus (15)
Trope. This figure is a very hostile form of mockery full of hate; that is, a very bitter joke.

123

Scaliger (III, lxxxviif)
Under *ironia*. This figure metaphorically applies false qualities in a case where it is known beyond doubt that they are false. . . . It may be, but is not always, ironic. This figure demands to be combined with the stylistic quality of *acre* or the bitter.

Peacham (37f)
Trope. A bitter kind of derision . . . to repress proud folly and wicked insolency.

EXAMPLES
Puttenham (190)
(Of a fat prisoner) I have gone a hunting many times, yet never took I such a swine before.

Peacham (38)
Thou which dost destroy the temple and build it again in three days, save thyself and come down from the cross.

Rufinianus
Sherry, Day

Iteratio

Cicero (*De Oratore*, III, liii, 203)
Scheme. Repetition of the proposition before drawing our formal conclusions.

Erasmus (25)
For plenitude of words. The use of different words to express the same thought. It serves to convey an appeal to the emotions.

Wilson (182)
Scheme. To repeat in a few words the sum of his saying.

Puttenham (236f)
Scheme. An earnest and hasty heaping up of speeches made by way of recapitulation . . . commonly in the end of every long tale and oration . . . a collection of all the former material points.

EXAMPLES

Wilson (182)
First, I will prove there is no cause that I should steal. Again, that I could not possibly at such a time steal, and last, that I stole not at all.

Hoskins (32)
You have heard of his pride, ambition, cosenage, robberies, mutinies, in the city, in the camp, in the country. What kinsman of his unabused, what friend undeceived, what companion uncorrupted can speak for him? Where can he live without shame? Where can he die with honour?

Quintilian

Judicatio
also known as *elogium*

Veltkirchius (98)
A part of an oration. A means to plenitude of matter.

Scaliger (III, xl)
Under *tractatio*. The poet passes a judgement upon his matter which is added on to a passage of description. It may include *sententiae*, or be accompanied by *exclamatio*. The poet may praise or criticize. We may have an *elogium* outside the poet's personal statement and implicit in the work itself.

EXAMPLE

Scaliger (III, xl)
They cannot slake their hearts with gazing upon his fearful eyes, his face, his chest shaggy with the hairs of a wild beast and those fires extinguished in their sockets. [An implicit criticism.]

Jusurandum (Orcos)
also known as *pariepsis*

Peacham (75)
Scheme. The speaker expresseth an oath for the better comfirmation

of something being affirmed or denied. . . . Most aptly . . . to confirm matters . . . by high and divine testimony.

EXAMPLES

Peacham (75)
I call heaven and earth to record against you this day, that you shall shortly perish from the land whereunto ye go over Jordan to possess it.
For God is my witness, whom I serve in my spirit in the Gospel of his son, that without ceasing I make mention of you always in my prayers.

Quintilian
Robortellus

Lamentatio (Threnos)
also known as *commiseratio, oictros*

Peacham (66f)
Scheme. The orator lamenteth some person or people for the misery they suffer, or the speaker his own calamity . . . it is most forcible and mighty to move pity and compassion in the hearer.

EXAMPLES

Peacham (66)
O that my head were full of water, and mine eyes a fountain of tears, that I might weep day and night, for the slain of the daughter of my people.

Peacham (67)
Why died not I in the birth? Why did I not perish as soon as I came out of the womb? Why set they me upon their knees? Why gave they me suck with their breasts?

Cicero
Sherry

Laudatio (Encomion)

Scaliger (III, cx)
Species under genus *laus*. The praise of perfection or perfect deeds, describing what has been added to natural virtue by art. This mode of speaking is not brief and simple but ornate, and its proper subjects are things which are above the common.

Peacham (155)
Scheme. The orator doth highly commend to his hearers some person or thing in respect of their worthy deserts and virtues. . . . By this figure we praise princes for their wisdom, clemency, mercy.

EXAMPLE
Peacham (155)
For if *Cornelius Pompey* had been five hundred years ago, such a man he was of whom being a young man and a Roman knight, the Senate might oftentimes have required aid and defence, whose noble acts with a most renowned victory both by land and sea had spread over all nations. . . . Whom the people of Rome had commended with singular honour, . . . when death had quenched envy, his noble acts should have flourished in glory of an eternal renown: whose virtues being bruited, should have given no place to doubts.

Quintilian

Libera vox (Parresia)
also known as *licentia*

Quintilian (IX, ii, 27)
Scheme. Free speech . . . only a figure when it is simulated and artfully designed. Freedom of speech may frequently be made a cloak for flattery.

Scaliger (III, lxvii)
Under *tractatio*. We imitate the characteristics of a free and open personality to inspire in the jury benevolence and mercy towards us.

Fraunce (76)
Scheme. A certain exclamation, when in the presence of those to whom otherwise we owe duty and reverence, we speak boldly and confidently.

Peacham (113)
Scheme. The orator speaking before those whom he feareth, or ought to reverence, and having somewhat to say that may either touch themselves, or those that they favour, preventeth the displeasure and offence that might be taken, as by craving pardon afore hand, and by showing the necessity of free speech in that behalf.

EXAMPLES

Fraunce (77)
I therefore say to thee, O just Judge, that I and only I was the worker of *Basilius'* death: they were these hands that gave unto him that poisonous potion, that brought death to him and loss to *Arcadia*.

Peacham (114)
I speak with great peril, I fear judges after what sort you may take my words, but for my continual desire that I have to maintain and augment your dignity, I pray and beseech you, that if my speech be either bitter or incredible unto you at the first hearing, yet that you would accept it without offence spoken of Marcus Cicero: Neither that you will reject it before I have plainly declared the whole unto you.

Ad Herennium, Cicero, Rutilius Lupus, Rufinianus
Melancthon, Susenbrotus, Talaeus, Wilson, Puttenham, Day

Locus (Topographia)

Quintilian (IX, ii, 44)
Scheme. The clear and vivid description of places.

Erasmus (54f)
To be used as an introduction to a narration. It gives the appearance of a place as if it was in sight, as if the place was real. The more unusual

these descriptions are the more pleasure they give, provided they are not wholly strange.

Susenbrotus (88)
Scheme. This is not a figure used only by poets, but even by historians and orators. . . . It tries to present the place to the hearers like a painting before spectators.

Peacham (141)
Scheme. An evident and true description of a place. . . . To this figure refer Cosmography by which is described countries, cities, towns, temples, palaces, castles, walls, gates, mountains, valleys, fields, orchards, gardens, fountains, dens, and all other manner of places.

EXAMPLES

Peacham (141)
Cicero describeth Syracusae, a city in Sicilia, and that excellently.
In Pliny there are descriptions of Acaia, Egypt, mount Etna, Africa, Alexandria, . . . Arabia, Armenia, Asia, Athens, Bithnia, Cyprus, Crete, Dalmatia, Gallatia, Hispania, Italia, the river Nilus, Pamphilia, the isle of Rhodes, the city of Rome, Sardinia, Sicilia, Thessalia and many others.

Melancthon, Sherry, Scaliger, Puttenham

Membrum (Colon)

Ad Herennium (IV, 26)
A part of a sentence, brief and complete, which does not express the entire thought but is in turn supplemented by another *colon* . . . it is neatest and most complete when composed of three *cola*.

Sherry (D$_v$)
Scheme. A member of the reason is so called when a thing is showed perfectly in few words the whole sentence not showed, but received again in another part. . . . This exornation may be made of two parts only, but the perfectest is made of three.

Scaliger (IV, xxv)
Scheme. *Colon* is a part of a periodic sentence with its own verb.

EXAMPLES

Sherry (D$_v$)
Thou didest both profit thine enemy and hurt thy friend.
Thou didest profit thine enemy, hurt thy friend, and didest no good to thyself.

Cicero, Quintilian, Rufinianus
Melancthon, Veltkirchius, Day

Necessitas (Anagkeon)

Quintilian (IX, ii, 106)
Scheme. The representation of the necessity of a thing.

Sherry (Dvi^v)
Scheme. When we confess the thing to be done but excuse it by necessity, either of person or time.

Scaliger (III, lxvi)
Under *tractatio*. When we carry the action back to its necessary causes, which are derived from nature, ethics, the law, time, place or age.

EXAMPLE

Sherry (Dvi^v)
I confess that this I did. But the woman that thou gavest me did deceive me.

Melancthon

Negando (Antiphrasis)
also known as *contrarium* (not to be confused with *antithesis*)

Quintilian (IX, ii, 47f)
Scheme. It derives its name from negation . . . and may be sustained at times through whole sections of our argument.

Susenbrotus (11)
Trope. For single words when by one word we mean its opposite.

Susenbrotus (16)
Trope. For sentences. A form of allegory when a word or expression is understood to mean its opposite.

Puttenham (191)
When we deride by plain and flat contradiction.

EXAMPLES

Puttenham (191)
(For a dwarf) See yonder giant.

Peacham (24)
You are always my friend (meaning *my enemy*).
You are a man of great judgment (signifying *unapt and unable to judge*).

Rufinianus
Scaliger, Day

Negatio (Apophasis)
also known as *depulsio*

Scaliger (III, lxxxix)
Under *irony*. The most natural of the ironic figures, the negative reply
. . . very like *occupatio*.

Fraunce (13)
Trope. A kind of irony, a denial or refusal to speak . . . when nevertheless we speak and tell all.

EXAMPLES

Scaliger (III, lxxxix)
I am not trying to disprove or refute what you say.

Fraunce (13)
I will not say that which I might.
I will not call you. . . .

Rufinianus, Fortunatianus

131

Nominatio (Onomatopoeia)
also known as *procreatio*

Quintilian (VIII, vi, 31)
Trope. The creation of a word . . . scarcely permissible to a Roman. It is true that many words were created in this way by the original founders of the language who adapted them to suit the sensation which they expressed.

Erasmus (31)
For plenitude of words. The coining of a name. This figure includes *paragoge*, the development of new words by analogy.

Susenbrotus (9f)
Trope. The making of a new word imitating the sound of what it signifies. Secondly, it includes all those words that we openly coin or adapt by necessity, although this latter is not properly a trope because there is no change of meaning

Puttenham (182)
Then also is the sense figurative when we devise a new name to anything consonant, as near as we can to the nature thereof . . . or as we give special names to the voices of dumb beasts.

Peacham (14f)
Trope. Maketh and feigneth a name to something, imitating the sound or voice of that it signifieth or else whereby he affecteth a word derived from the name of a person, or from the original of the thing which it doth express. And this form of feigning, and framing names is used diverse ways. First, by imitation of sound, . . . Secondly, by imitation of voices, . . . Thirdly by the derivation from the original, . . . Fourthly, by composition, as when we put two words together and make of them but one [see under COMPOSITIO], . . . Fifthly by reviving antiquity. Touching this part I will refer the reader to Chaucer and Gower, and to the new Shepherds Calendar, a most singular imitation of ancient speech . . . [sixthly] when we signify the imitation of another man's property or fashion.

132

EXAMPLES

Puttenham (182)
Flashing of lightning, clashing of blades, clinking of fetters.

Peacham (15f)
1. A hurliburly, creaking.
2. The roaring of lions, the bellowing of bulls.
3. Luds-town of Lud, now London.
4. Scholarlike, thickskin, pinchpenny, bellygod (glutton), pickthank (flatterer).
5. [See above].
6. I cannot court it, I cannot Italian it.

Ad Herennium
Melancthon, Wilson, Day

Notatio (Ethopoeia)
also known as *circonstatio*

Ad Herennium (IV, 63ff)
When we describe the qualities proper to a particular nature or type
. . . By such delineation anyone's ruling passion can be brought into
the open.

Cicero (*Orator*, xl, 138)
Scheme. To describe the talk and character of particular persons.

Erasmus (51)
Character sketches. . . . The material is drawn from all circumstances,
especially . . . culture, speech, language, . . . age, . . . fortune, . . . disposition.

Wilson (187)
Scheme. We describe the manners of men, when we set them forth in
their kind what they are.

EXAMPLE

Wilson (187)
There is no such pinch penny on live as this good fellow is. He will
not lose the paring of his nails. His hair is never rounded for sparing
of money, one pair of shoes serveth him a twelve month, he is shod
with nails like a horse. He hath been known by his coat this thirty
winter. He spent once a groat at good ale, being forced through company, and taken short at his word, whereupon he hath taken such
conceit since that time, that it hath almost cost him his life.

Rufinianus
Veltkirchius, Sherry, Scaliger

Nugatio (Tautologia)

Quintilian (VIII, iii, 50)
The repetition of a word or phrase. If it is deliberately employed it is
a scheme. . . . It may sometimes be regarded as a fault.

Scaliger (IV, xxxii)
Scheme. The repetition of the same word carelessly and without attention to taste.

Peacham (42)
Vice. Excessive repetition in *repetitio*.

Peacham (49)
Vice. Wearisome repetition of one word in *traductio*.

Peacham (193)
Vice. A wearisome repetition of all one word [in *expolitio*].

EXAMPLE

Peacham (49)
If you have a friend, keep your friend, for an old friend is to be preferred before a new friend, this I say to you as your friend.

Aquila
Melancthon, Veltkirchius, Sherry, Puttenham

Obsecratio (Deisis)

also known as *obtestatio* (not to be confused with *asseveratio*)

Peacham (71)
Scheme. By which the orator expresseth his most earnest request, petition, or prayer.

EXAMPLES

Peacham (71)
O Chremes I beseech thee for God's sake and for our old friendship's sake, which hath continued ever since we were children which time hath also increased, and for thy only daughter's sake, and my son's whom I have committed wholly to thy government, help me in this matter.

If innocency may deserve favour, if misery may move to pity, or prayers prevail with men: let your mercy for God's sake relieve misery, and your compassion extend to us that are ready to perish.

Cicero
Melancthon

Occupatio (Paralepsis)

also known as *occultatio, praeteritio, negatio* (not to be confused with *apophasis*)

Ad Herennium (IV, 37)
When we cut short or refuse to continue or say nothing of most of the subject we are discussing. . . . Useful if we can imply by omission something which we could not prove by saying.

Susenbrotus (82f)
Scheme. When we pretend to pass over something, not to know it or not to wish to say it when it is something we wish above all to say, or when we say in passing what we deny we want to say at all.

Fraunce (13)
Trope. A kind of irony, a kind of pretended omitting or letting slip of

K   135

that which indeed we elegantly note out in the very show of praetermission.

Peacham (130f)
Scheme. When the orator feigneth and maketh as though he would say nothing in some matter, when, notwithstanding he speaketh most of all, or when he saith something: in saying he will not say it.

EXAMPLES

Fraunce (14)
To tell you what pitiful mishaps fell to the young Prince of Macedon his cousin, I should too much fill your ears with strange horrors: neither will I stay upon those laboursome adventures, nor loathsome misadventures, to which and through his fortune and courage conducted him.

Peacham (131)
I will make no mention of his drunken banquets nightly, and his watching with bawds, dicers, whore masters. I will not name his losses, his luxurity, and staining of his honesty.

Cicero, Quintilian, Aquila, Fortunatianus
Trapezuntius, Melancthon, Veltkirchius, Sherry, Puttenham, Day, Hoskins

Ominatio

Peacham (90)
Scheme. The orator fortelleth the likeliest effect to follow of some evil cause.

EXAMPLES

Peacham (90)
If thou followest these purposes, believe me thou canst not long continue.
Therefore thy poverty cometh upon thee as one that travelleth by the way, and thy necessity like an armed man.

Optatio

Wilson (152)
For the moving of the affections. In speaking against an evil man, and wishing somewhat thereupon, a jest may seem delightful.

Peacham (72)
Scheme. The orator expresses his desire by wishing to God or men . . . to signify our desires by wishing, which we cannot accomplish by our power.

EXAMPLES
Wilson (152)
Demonides having crooked feet, lost on a time both his shoes, whereupon he made his prayer to God, that his shoes might serve his feet, that had stolen them away.

Peacham (72)
I would the immortal gods had granted that we might rather have given thanks to Servius Sulpitius being alive, than now to examine his honours being dead.
I would to God, that my Lord were with the prophet that is in Samaria.

Cicero, Quintilian

Ordo (Catacosmesis)

Wilson (208)
Scheme. Of two sorts, the one is when the worthier is preferred and set before. The second is, when in amplification, the weightiest words are set last, and in diminishing the same are set foremost.

Peacham (118f)
Scheme. A meet placing of words among themselves whereof there be two kinds, the one when the worthiest word is set first, which order is natural. . . . The other kind of order is artificial, and in form contrary to this, as when the worthiest or weightiest word is set last: for the cause of amplifying

137

EXAMPLES

Wilson (208)
With what look, with what face, with what heart dare thou do such a deed?

Peacham (118)
God and man, men and women, sun and moon, life and death (natural).

Quintilian

Partitio

Peacham (124f)
Scheme. A form of speech by which the orator divideth the whole into parts. . . . Serveth to minister plenty and variety of matter.

EXAMPLE

Peacham (124)
Every nation hath his team and his plough to get his living, his bed to take his rest, some fruit of his labour for his friend, his bow and his spear for his enemy, his bow to meet him far off, and his spear to wound him nigh at hand, mourning at burials, mirth at marriage and religious worship in their temples. (Here the general custom of nations is the whole which as you see is divided into certain parts.)

Quintilian
Trapezuntius

Perclusio (Cataplexis)
also known as *comminatio*

Scaliger (III, lxii)
Under *tractatio*. A threat.

Peacham (79f)
Scheme. The orator denounceth a threatening against some person, people, city . . . or country, containing and declaring the certainty or likelihood of plagues, or punishments.

EXAMPLES

Peacham (80)
Yet forty days and Nineveh shall be destroyed.
Woe be to you that are full, for ye shall hunger: Woe be to you that laugh, for ye shall wail and weep.

Quintilian

Percontatio (Exetasis)

Cicero (*De Oratore*, III, liii, 203)
Scheme. To enquire of others and set forth our own opinion.

Wilson (184)
Scheme. We do ask because we would chide, and set forth our grief with more vehemency.

Scaliger (IV, xlii)
Scheme. When we make inquiries about what we do not know.

EXAMPLE

Wilson (184)
How long, Catiline, wilt thou abuse our sufferance? How long with this rage and madness of thine go about to deceive us?

Quintilian

Percursio (Epiprochasmos)
also known as *collectio*

Susenbrotus (71)
Scheme. A form of *congeries*, a rapid summary at the conclusion of the argument.

139

EXAMPLE

Susenbrotus (71)
The fruits of the spirits are charity, joy, peace, mercy, benevolence, goodness, faith, compassion, temperance.

Cicero, Aquila

Permissio

also known as *concessio* (not to be confused with *epitropis*)

Quintilian (IX, ii, 25)
Scheme. When we leave some things to the judgment of the jury, or even in some cases of our opponents.

Fraunce (102)
Scheme. Sufferance is when we mockingly give leave to do somewhat.

Puttenham (226)
Scheme. When we will not seem, either for manner sake or to avoid tediousness, to trouble the judge or hearer with all that we could say. . . . We refer the rest to their consideration.

EXAMPLES

Wilson (205)
Take your pleasure for a time, and do what you list, a time will come when account shall be made.

Fraunce (103)
If you seek the victory, take it, and if you list, triumph: have you all the reason of the world, and with me remain all the imperfections?

Cicero
Trapezuntius, Melancthon, Talaeus, Scaliger

Permutatio (Enallage)

also known as *antiptosis, metallage, allage*

Quintilian (IX, iii, 6ff)
Scheme. The interchange of grammatical forms . . . the genders of nouns, the active or passive forms of verbs, the number of nouns . . . a verb for a noun . . . the interchange of tenses. There is a figure corresponding to every form of solecism.

Erasmus (25f)
For plenitude of words. Variety is gained by a small change in the word itself, such as a change from one part or speech to another; for example infinitive to noun . . . or a change of the form of the same part of speech. . . . Tense, mood, declension and conjugation can be varied.

Puttenham (171)
Scheme. A working by exchange . . . using one case for another. . . . We [English] having no such variety of accidents, have little or no use of this figure.

EXAMPLE
Sherry (Bviii)
Me think it is so.

Peacham (1577, Hiii)
He is condemned of murder (instead of *for murder*).

Peacham (Hiii^v)
It is a wicked daughter that despiseth her mother (instead of *she is*). The fowl which fly in winter season (instead of *the fowls*).

Peacham (Hiv)
What thing more worthy may be written of Cicero to Cicero (instead of *of me unto thee*).

Susenbrotus, Scaliger

Perseverantia (Epimone)

Puttenham (225)
Scheme. When poets do link their staves together with one verse running throughout the whole song by equal distance . . . mostly the first verse of the staff.

Peacham (70)
Scheme. The speaker continueth and persisteth in the same cause, much after one form of speech. . . . By this form of speech the greatness of the desire is signified.

EXAMPLES
Puttenham (225)
Sidney's poem 'My true love hath my heart and I have his' begins and ends with this verse.

Peacham (70)
If there be fifty righteous within the city wilt thou destroy, and not spare the place for the fifty righteous that are therein?

Praecisio (Aposiopesis)
also known as *reticentia, obticentia, interruptio* (not to be confused with *paraposiopesis*), *cognata*

Quintilian (IX, ii, 54)
Scheme. Used to indicate passion or anger . . . or to give an impression of anxiety or scruple . . . or as a means of transition to another topic.

Quintilian (IX, iii, 60)
What is suppressed is uncertain or would require an explanation of some length to show what it is.

Talaeus (80f)
Scheme. A sentence which has been begun and is halted in midcourse so that the part which is not expressed may be readily understood.

Scaliger (III, lxxvii)
Under *eclipsis*. When we cut ourselves short, a device leading to brevity. *Aposiopesis* is when we stop without a word of explanation or exclamation of surprise—we simply leave off.

Fraunce (80)
Scheme. When the course of a speech is in such sort staid, that some part thereof not uttered, is nevertheless perceived [see under DETRAC-TIO].

Peacham (118)
Scheme. The orator through some affection, as either of fear, anger,
sorrow, bashfulness or such like, breaketh off his speech before it be all
ended. . . . The use of this form of speech . . . is to signify by half what
the whole meaneth, . . . to raise a sufficient suspicion without danger of
the adversary.

EXAMPLES

Fraunce (80f)
> Virtue awake, beauty but beauty is,
> I may, I must, I can, I will, I do
> Leave following that, which it is gain to miss
> Let her go: soft, but here she comes: go to
> Unkind I love you not, o me, that eye
> Doth make my heart give to my tongue the lie.

Peacham (118)
How doth the child Ascanius, whom timely Troy to thee—
I am loth to utter that with my mouth which is now in my mind.
Modesty bids me stay.

Ad Herennium, Cicero, Aquila
Trapezuntius, Melancthon, Veltkirchius, Susenbrotus, Puttenham, Day

Praeexpositio (Proecthesis)

Quintilian (IX, ii, 106)
Pointing out what ought to have been done, and then what actually
has been done.

Scaliger (III, lxxii)
Under *tractatio*. This figure contains first a description of something
which has been done or which has not been done. And secondly we
insert the arguments against the deed or against its feebleness or failure.
Praeexpositio is therefore a kind of conclusion to the contrary.

Peacham (102f)
Scheme. The speaker defendeth by his answer, containing a reason of that which he hath said or done, proving that he ought not be blamed. . . . This figure is a form of confutation.

EXAMPLES

Peacham (103)
Is it lawful to do good or evil on the Sabbath? To save a man or to destroy him?
Which of you having one sheep, if it fall into a pit on the Sabbath, will not pull it out and raise it up?

Rutilius Lupus
Veltkirchius

Praemunitio

Cicero (*De Oratore*, III, liii, 204)
Scheme. We may defend ourselves by anticipating objections to some point we propose to make later.

Wilson (187)
Scheme. A buttress is a sense made for that, which we purpose to hold up, or go about to compass.

EXAMPLE

Wilson (187)
I hope my Lords, both to persuade this man by reason, and to have your judgment in this matter. For whereas it is a sour thing to be justly accused for breaking friendship, then assuredly if one be wrongfully slandered, a man had need to look about him.

Quintilian, Rufinianus
Scaliger

Praeparatio (Etiologia)

Quintilian (IX, ii, 17)
Scheme. A form of *praesumptio*, whereby we state fully why we are going to do something or have done it.

Puttenham (228)
Scheme. For better persuasion to tell the cause that moves us to say thus or thus: or else we would fortify our allegations by rendering reasons to every one.

Peacham (184f)
Scheme. The orator joineth reason or cause to a proposition uttered . . . the reason joined unto it as an authentic seal to an evidence: and it serveth to confirmation and confutation.

EXAMPLES

Puttenham (229)
    And for her beauty's praise, no wight that with her wars:
    For when she comes she shows herself like sun among the stars.

Peacham (184)
Look what wit or eloquence I have, Judges, Archia may justly challenge it to himself: for he was the first and principal, that caused me to follow these manners of studies.
He brought me forth into a place of liberty, he brought me forth even because he had a favour unto me.

Cicero, Rutilius Lupus
Trapezuntius, Melancthon, Susenbrotus, Wilson, Day

Praeposteratio (Hysteron proteron)

Susenbrotus (32)
Scheme. When we give the first place in the passage to what chronologically occurred second. . . . This is an alteration of order in the meaning of the statement, not in the words.

Sherry (Bviii)
Scheme. When it that is done afterwards, is set in speaking in the former place.

Peacham (141)
Vice of style. When the circumstances be preposterously placed, as to rehearse that last, which was first done.

EXAMPLES
Sherry (Bviii)
Pluck off my boots and spurs.

Puttenham (170)
When we had climbed the cliffs, and were ashore.

Day

Praescriptio

Scaliger (III, liv)
Under *tractatio*. A species of *diatyposis*, *praescriptio* lists what may be usefully stated along with naming the subject, and resembles other figures of moderation and emendation. For example, in describing the fortunes of men we may mention that they are strong, happy and particularly blessed.

EXAMPLE
Scaliger (III, liv)
And happy Tolumnius, the next chosen by Latius from Laurentian fields.

Praesumptio (Prolepsis)
also known as *parasceue, propergasia*

Quintilian (IX, ii, 16f)
Scheme. We forestall objections later [known as *occupatio*, see under ANTE OCCUPATIO] . . . or defend by anticipation [see under PRAE-MUNITIO] . . . or anticipate by confessing something we can afford to

concede . . . or by predicting something . . . or correcting ourselves . . . or stating fully our reasons [see under PRAEPARATIO].

Susenbrotus (83)
Scheme. When we anticipate objections to our argument before they can be put forward [see under ANTE OCCUPATIO].

Scaliger (III, xlix)
Under *tractatio*. When the poet states all those aspects of a character that are not immediately obvious. . . . He may do it in two ways: the indirect, whereby the character is described metaphorically and by a third person, or the direct, in *sermocinatio* form when the character reveals himself through his own speech. This is particularly effective if the character is dead or non-human.

Peacham (1577, Fi^v)
Scheme. When a general word going before, is afterwards divided into parts.

Puttenham (167f)
Scheme. . . . A manner of speaking purporting at the first blush a defect which afterward is supplied. . . . . The first proposition in a sort defective, and of imperfect sense, till ye come by division to explain and enlarge it.

EXAMPLES

Peacham (Fi^v)
We were both in great sorrow, I for the loss of my dear friend, and he for fear of banishment.
Three sisters did sing, the eldest the base, the middlemost the mean, and the youngest . . . the treble.

Puttenham (168)
       That our long love may lead us to agree:
       Me since I may not wed you as my wife,
       To serve you as a mistress all my life:
       Ye that ye may not me for your husband have,
       To claim me for your servant and your slave.

Rutilius Lupus, Rufinianius
Melancthon, Day

Prohibitio (Apagoresis)

Scaliger (III, lxxxiii)
Under *eclipsis*. A statement designed to inhibit someone from doing
something. We may use an example, a comparison, an excuse.

EXAMPLE

Scaliger (III, lxxxiii)
If it is the wrath of the gods, not even Drances can atone for this by
death.

Quintilian

Promissio (Euche)

also known as *precatio, votum*

Scaliger (III, lxiii)
Under *tractatio*. The promise, the opposite of *perclusio* [the threat]. If
it is a genuine promise it is not a figure at all. If it is a figure, it is a part
of the passage which enlarges or expands the initial proposition.

Peacham (67)
Scheme. The orator or speaker expresses a solemn promise or vow;
either made with condition, or rising from some vehement affection.

EXAMPLES

Peacham (67)
If God will be with me, and will keep me in this journey which I go,
and will give me bread to eat, and cloth to put on, so that I come again
unto my father in safety. Then shall the Lord be my God, and this stone
which I have set up as a pillar, shall be God's house, and of all that thou
shalt give me, will I give the tenth unto thee.

Peacham (68)
An example of a vow rising from affection, and without condition is expressed in the Psalm 132.
[Surely I will not come into the tabernacle of my house nor go up into my bed; I will not give sleep to mine eyes, or slumber to mine eyelids, until I find out a place for the Lord.]

Cicero, Quintilian, Rufinianus
Sherry

Pronominatio (Antonomasia)
also known as *nominis permutatio*

Quintilian (VIII, vi, 29)
Trope. It substitutes something else for a proper name. Very common in poets: it may be done in two ways: by the substitution of an epithet as equivalent to the name which it replaces . . . or by indicating the most striking characteristics of an individual.

Erasmus (27)
For plenitude of words. A method of varying the diction by a change of name.

Puttenham (181)
A manner of naming persons or things . . . not by way of misnaming but by a convenient difference such as is true or esteemed and likely to be true.

Peacham (22)
Trope. A naming or the changing of a name. . . . The orator for a proper name putteth another, as some name of dignity, office, profession, science or trade.

EXAMPLES
Wilson (175)
Blessed are they, whose sins be not imputed unto them (David).

Puttenham (181f)
Vallois . . . the name of his house (the French king).
The peaceable (her majesty Elizabeth).

Peacham (22)
Your Majesty, your Highness.

Peacham (23)
The philosopher (Aristotle), the Psalmograph (David).
A Cato (a grave man), a Solomon (a wise man).

Ad Herennium
Melancthon, Susenbrotus, Sherry, Scaliger, Day

Propositio
also known as *prolepsis* (not to be confused with *praesumptio*).

Cicero (*De Oratore*, III, liii, 203)
Scheme. We may set forth in advance what we propose to say.

Susenbrotus (28)
Scheme. A general statement which precedes the division of this general proposition into parts.

Wilson (182)
Scheme. A short rehearsal of that, whereof we mind to speak.

Peacham (192)
Scheme. Comprehendeth in few words, the sum of the matter whereof we presently intend to speak.

EXAMPLES

Wilson (182)
I will tell you there is none hath a worse name than this fellow, none hath been so often in trouble.

Peacham (192)
I have now to speak of the excellent and singular virtues of Pompeius. And because the decree of the Senate is not yet written, I will show you as much thereof as I can call to remembrance.

Quintilian

Proverbium (Parimia)
also known as *adagium*

Susenbrotus (13f)
Trope. A celebrated or well-known saying . . . common to everyone, commended equally for its antiquity and its wisdom.

Scaliger (III, lxxxiv)
Under *allegory*. It concerns events or seasons but is not restricted to a particular place. . . . It is abstruse not self-declaring . . . and to display his wit the poet may expound it.

Peacham (29)
Trope. A sentence or form of speech much used and commonly known and also excellent for the similitude and the signification: to which two things are necessarily required, the one, that it be renowned, and much spoken of as a sentence in every man's mouth. The other, that it be witty.

EXAMPLES

Puttenham (189)
As the old cock crows so doth the chick.
Totness is turned French.

Peacham (30)
The tumbling stone doth seldom gather moss.
The sweetest rose hath his thorn.

Quintilian, Aquila
Melancthon, Veltkirchius, Sherry, Day

Provocatio (Proclesis)

Robortellus (49ᵛ)
This figure provokes. . . . It suits a speaker with boldness, persistence and confidence.

Peacham (83)
Scheme. A form of speech . . . which provokes the adversary to the conflict of the controversy, and that either by a vehement accusation, or by a confident offer of justification.

EXAMPLES

Peacham (83)
Is it for fear of thee that I will accuse thee, or go with thee into judgment? Is not thy wickedness great? and thine ungratious deeds abominable? for thou hast taken the pledge from thy brother for nought, and spoiled the clothes of the naked.
Which of you can rebuke me of sin?

Purgatio (Dichaeologia)

Susenbrotus (85)
Scheme. When we maintain the justice of our cause and defend our cause as equitable.

Scaliger (III, lxvii)
A mode of conducting a speech. When we confess to some deed and follow this by an explanation of how it occurred, the causes which led to it and the necessity of doing it.

Wilson (200)
Scheme. Sometimes we excuse a fault, and accuse the reporters.

Peacham (115)
Scheme. The orator defendeth his cause by equity, or excuseth it by necessity, or else doth extenuate it by alleging some other occasion.

EXAMPLES

Puttenham (230)
And said it not, but by misgovernment.

Peacham (115)
I forsook my friend, but the laws compelled me: I kept friendship most faithfully, as long as the laws permitted me, and now I am not cast off by will, but by force of law.

Ad Herennium, Cicero, Rutilius Lupus, Quintilian
Melancthon, Day

Quaestium (Pysma)

Melancthon (*Institutiones*, Div)
Scheme. When we use the interrogative to underline emotions such as admiration, determination and indignation.

Peacham (106f)
Scheme. A figure by which the orator doth demand many times together, and use many questions in one place, whereby he maketh his speech very sharp and vehement. . . . It serveth . . . to move affections and . . . should not be used to deceive the hearer by the multitude of questions.

EXAMPLES

Peacham (107)
In what place did he speak with them? with whom did he speak? did he hire them? whom did he hire, and by whom? To what end, or how much did he give them?
Will the Lord absent himself for ever, and will he be no more entreated? Is his mercy clean gone forever? and is his promise come utterly to an end for evermore? hath God forgotten to be gracious?

Aquila, Fortunatianus

Querimonia (Memphis)

Peacham (65)
Scheme. The orator maketh a complaint and craveth help.

EXAMPLES

Peacham (65f)
Why standest thou so far O lord, and hidest thyself in the needful time
of trouble? The ungodly for his own lust doth persecute the poor.
For thy sake also are we killed all the day long, and are counted as
sheep appointed to be slain.

Ratiocinatio

Ad Herennium (IV, 23)
We ask ourselves the reason for each statement we make, and seek the
meaning of each successive affirmation.

Susenbrotus (76)
Scheme. When we expand the matter by conjecture to some image or
picture, or lavishly, by describing all the circumstances relating to it.

Sherry (Dii^v)
Scheme. By the which we ourselves are a reason of ourself, wherefore
everything should be spoken, and that oftentimes we demand of ourselves a declaration of every proposition.

EXAMPLE

Sherry (Dii^{v}f)
This was well ordained by our elders to deprive no king of his life whom
they had taken in battle. Why so? For the power which fortune had
given us is to consume in the punishment of them whom the same
fortune a little before had set in highest degree, were against reason.
Yea, but he brought a great army against you? I will not remember it.
Why so? For it is the point of a valiant man such as intend for the
victory, them to count enemies: such as be overcome, those to count
men: so that fortitude may diminish war, humanity increase peace.

But if he had overcome, would he have done so? Verily he would not have been so wise. Why should ye spare him then? Because such folly I am wont to despise, not to follow.

Cicero, Quintilian
Erasmus

Recordatio (Anamnesis)

Peacham (76)
Scheme. The speaker calling to remembrance matters past, doth make a recital of them. Sometime matters of sorrow . . . Sometime with joy.

EXAMPLES

Peacham (76)
> Oh happy (welaway) and overhappy had I been
> If never Trojan ship alas, my country shore had seen.

By the rivers of Babel we sat and wept there, when we remembered Sion.

I will remember the works of the Lord, and call to mind thy wonders of old time.

Rutilius, Quintilian
Trapezuntius, Scaliger

Redditio (Prosapodosis)

Cicero (*De Oratore*, III, liv, 207)
This figure backs up each detail of a *distributio* [the proposition divided into all its parts] with a reason.

Hoskins (46)
Overthroweth no part of the division, but returneth some reason to each member . . . this affirms and keeps all sides up.

EXAMPLE

Hoskins (46)
Heretofore I have accused the sea, condemned the pirates, and hated
my evil fortune that deprived me of thee. But now thyself art the sea,
thyself the pirate, and thy will the evil fortune.
Time at one instant seeming short and long to them: short in the
pleasingness of such presence, long in the stay of their desires.

Rutilius Lupus, Quintilian, Aquila
Sherry

Reditus ad propositum

Cicero (*De Oratore*, III, liii, 203)
A neat and elegant return to the main theme after a digression.

Wilson (182)
Scheme. When we have made a digression, we may declare our return,
and show that whereas we have roved a little, we will now keep us
within our bounds.

Redundantia (Pleonasmos)
also known as *superabundantia*

Quintilian (VIII, iii, 53f)
Vice. When we overload our style with a superfluity of words. . . .
Sometimes the form of pleonasm may have a pleasing effect when
used for emphasis.

Susenbrotus (29)
Scheme. When we have a superfluity of words which nevertheless
gives grace to the speech . . . in the interest of either vehemence or
exaggeration.

Puttenham (257)
Vice. Too full speech.

Peacham (1577, Fii)
Scheme. When there be more words heaped upon a construction, than be necessary.

EXAMPLES
Puttenham (257)
For ever may my true love live and never die.

Peacham (Fii)
I saw your daughter Proserpine, with the same eyes.
Antiocus was sorry in his mind.

Aquila
Sherry, Scaliger, Day

Reduplicatio (Anadiplosis)
also known as *palilogia* (not to be confused with *heratio*), *duplicatio*

Susenbrotus (50)
Scheme. When the last word of the preceding unit is repeated at the beginning of the unit of speech following.

Fraunce (36)
Scheme. In diverse sentences. . . . When the same sound is repeated in the end of the sentence going before and in the beginning of the sentence following after.

Peacham (46f)
Scheme. The last word of the first clause is the beginning of the second . . . and doth serve . . . to add a certain increase in the second member.

Hoskins (12)
A repetition in the end of the former sentence and beginning of the next . . . in speech there is no repetition without importance.

EXAMPLES
Fraunce (37)

> O stealing time, the subject of delay,
> Delay the rack of unrefrained desire.

157

Peacham (46)
> Now followeth fair Assur
> Assur trusting to his steed.

Hoskins (12)
Why lived I, alas? Alas, which loved I? To die wretched, and to be the example of heaven's hate. And hate and spare not, for the worst blow is stricken.

Cicero, Aquila, Rufinianus
Melancthon, Talaeus, Sherry, Scaliger, Puttenham, Day

Refractio (Anaclasis)
also known as *antistasis*

Rufinianus (72)
Scheme. Repetition of the same word with a contrary meaning.

Sherry (Dvi^v)
Scheme. That is the turning back again of a word into a contrary signification.

EXAMPLE
Sherry (Dvi^v)
I know king Ezechias that all this life is but bitterness, but I pray thee give me such bitterness.

Rutilius Lupus, Quintilian

Regressio (Epanodos)
also known as *digestio, sinanthesis*

Quintilian (IX, iii, 35f)
Scheme. A form of repetition which simultaneously reiterates things that have already been said, and draws distinctions between them. . . . Nor are words only repeated to reaffirm the same meaning, but the repetition may serve to mark a contrast.

Susenbrotus (82)
Scheme. When we repeat the initial proposition but with a different significance, and something different is meant when it is analysed into parts.

Peacham (129)
Scheme. A figure which iterateth by parts, the whole spoken before, signifying a certain diversity in the parts which are divided.

EXAMPLES

Peacham (129)

> Iphitus and Pelias, that time with me fled out,
> Iphitus opprest with age, and Pelias Ulisses wound made
>   come behind.

For we are unto God the sweet savour of Christ in them that are saved, and in them which perish, to one the savour of death unto death, to the other, the savour of life unto life.

Cicero, Rufinianus
Melancthon, Wilson, Scaliger, Puttenham, Day, Hoskins

Regressio (Epanodos)

Talaeus (66)
Scheme. When we repeat the same sound in the beginning and middle of a unit or in the middle and the end.

Fraunce (46)
Scheme. Turning to the same sound, when one and the same sound is repeated in the beginning and middle, or middle and end.

EXAMPLES

Fraunce (47)

> To be in things past bounds of wit, fools, if they be not fools.
> Hear then, but then with wonder hear, see, but adoring see.

Rejectio (Apodixis)

Rufinianus (58)
Scheme. When we reject some point in the case against us as unworthy to have been put forward, to have been asked of us or demanded of the jury.

Wilson (186f)
Scheme. When we lay such faults from us, as our enemies would charge us withall, saying it is folly to think any such thing, much more to speak it.

Peacham (185)
Scheme. When the orator rejecteth the objection or argument of his adversaries as things needless, absurd, false, or impertinent to the purpose, as proceeding from folly, or framed by malice, or invented by subtlety.

EXAMPLES

Wilson (187)
Nay, it is thou, it is thou man and none other that sets Caesar on work, to seek the slaughter of his country.

Peacham (185)
Would any wise man ever have so said? Were not ignorance the cause of this opinion, folly could not be the fruit.

Quintilian
Melancthon, Scaliger

Repetitio

Scaliger (III, xli)
Under *tractatio*. The generic term for all forms of repetition. . . . Repetition is an instrument of proportion for gauging the concordance between the similar and the dissimilar; that is, in which aspects the dissimilar are similar.

Repetitio (Anaphora)
also known as *relatio, adjectio, epanaphora* and *epibole*

Cicero (De Oratore, III, liv, 206)
Scheme. The same word may be repeated at the beginning of a sentence.

Fraunce (40)
Scheme. A bringing back of the same sound, when the same sound is iterated in the beginning of the sentence.

Puttenham (198)
Scheme. When we make one word begin . . . and lead the dance to many verses in suit.

EXAMPLES
Fraunce (41)

> Old age is wise, and full of constant truth,
> Old age well stayed from ranging humors lives,
> Old age hath known, whatever was in youth,
> Old age o'ercome the greater honour gives.

Peacham (41f)
The Lord sitteth above the water floods. The Lord remaineth a king for ever. The Lord shall give strength unto his people. The Lord shall give his people the blessing of peace.

Hoskins (13)
You whom my choice hath made the gods of my safety, you that nature made the lodestar of comfort.

Ad Herennium, Rutilius Lupus, Quintilian, Aquila, Rufinianus Melancthon, Susenbrotus, Talaeus, Sherry, Wilson, Scaliger, Day

Reprehensio (Metanoia)
also known as *aphorismon* (see also CORRECTIO)

Quintilian (IX, ii, 18)
Scheme. To qualify the meaning we give to a word, as in 'Citizens, if I may call you by that name'.

Quintilian (IX, ii, 60)
Scheme. We may feign repentance for what we have said.

Peacham (173)
Scheme. *Metanoia* is comprehended under Correction, and it is . . . a description of things by reprehension. . . . But of other authors it is taken for a form of speech by which the orator repenting himself of some word or saying past, by fault of memory or want of due consideration, craveth leave to resume it . . . and to place a fitter word instead thereof.

EXAMPLES

Peacham (173)
He sheweth himself a man amongst his enemies, nay a lion.
We are fools that do presume to compare Drusus Africanus, Pompeius and ourselves with Clodius.

Cicero, Rutilius Lupus, Rufinianus, Fortunatianus
Day

Restrictio

Peacham (131)
Scheme. When of the general word going before, a part afterward is excepted, or when of things first expressed, some alteration is noted.

EXAMPLES

Peacham (131)
We are afflicted on every side, yet we are not in distress: in poverty, yet not overcome of poverty: we are persecuted, but not forsaken: cast down but we perish not.

Peacham (132)
I have seen the wicked in great prosperity and flourishing like the green bay tree, yea he passed away and lo he was gone, I sought him but he could not be found.

Resumptio (Epanalepsis)

Cicero (De Oratore, III, liv, 206)
Scheme. The sentence may be made to open and close with the same phrase.

Susenbrotus (30f)
Scheme. When after some words or phrases we repeat the initial word or phrase of our speech for clarity or for some other reason.

Susenbrotus (49)
Scheme. When we begin and end a unit with the same expression.

Scaliger (IV, xxix)
Scheme. The repetition of a word or sound with a few sounds interposed between the first and the second instance.

Fraunce (45)
Scheme. When the same sound is iterated in the beginning and ending.

Peacham (46)
Scheme. A form of speech which doth both begin and also end a sentence with one and the same word . . . to place a word of importance in the beginning of the sentence to be considered, and in the end to be remembered.

EXAMPLES

Fraunce (45)
       They love indeed, who quake to say, they love.
The thoughts are but overflowings of the mind, and the tongue is but a servant of the thoughts.

Peacham (46)
At midnight thou wentest out of thy house, and returnedst again at midnight.
O ye careless cities, after years, and days shall ye be brought in fear, O ye careless cities.

Rutilius Lupus, Quintilian, Aquila, Rufinianus
Trapezuntius, Erasmus, Melancthon, Talaeus, Puttenham, Day, Hoskins

Reticentia
(not to be confused with *praecisio*)

Wilson (199)
Scheme. Whisht, is when we bid them hold their peace, that have least cause to speak, and can do little good with their talking.

EXAMPLE

Wilson (199)
Diogenes being upon the sea among a number of naughty packs in a great storm ... when diverse of these wicked fellows cried out ... 'Whisht' quoth Diogenes 'for by God's mother, if God himself knew you be here, you were like to be drowned every mother's son of you'.

Cicero, Quintilian

Reversio (Anastrophe)
also known as *præpostere, inversio, epanastrophe* and *hypallage* (not to be confused with *metonymia*)

Quintilian (VIII, vi, 65)
Trope. The transposition of two words only . . . a reversal of order.

Susenbrotus (31)
Scheme. A preposterous ordering in which the word which follows should be first.

Day (82)
Scheme. A preposterous inversion of words besides their common course.

EXAMPLES

Sherry (Bviii)
He fell from off the wall (for *he fell off from the wall*).

Day (82)
For faults, no man liveth without.
Long when he had confusedly thus lived.

Cicero
Melancthon, Sherry, Scaliger

Rogatio (Antipophora)

also known as *responsio, suggestio, objectio, disputatio, subjectio, hypophora* (not to be confused with a more limited figure known as *subjectio* or *hypophora*)

Quintilian (IX, ii, 15)
Scheme. To ask a question and not to wait for a reply but to subjoin the reply at once yourself.

Susenbrotus (58f)
Scheme. When we reply to our own question. We may do this in three ways: we may ourselves make an objection our listeners might make and reply to this objection [see under SUBJECTIO]: we may simulate a conversation with our adversary providing his replies: . . . we may pretend to deliberate a point through various questions and answers, replying to objections one by one.

Wilson (183f)
Scheme. By asking . . . and answering the question ourself, we much commend the matter, and make it appear very pleasant.

Peacham (107f)
Scheme. The orator answereth to his own demand.

EXAMPLES

Peacham (107f)
Whom hast thou defied and blasphemed? against whom hast thou lifted up thy voice, and exalted thy proud looks? Even against the holy one of Israel.
Shall we continue in sin, that grace may abound? God forbid.

Ad Herennium, Cicero, Rufinianus, Fortunatianus
Trapezuntius, Melancthon, Sherry, Puttenham, Day

Scurra (Cacemphaton)
(see also TURPILOQUUM)

Quintilian (VIII, iii, 44)
Vice. The employment of language to which perverted usage has given an obscene meaning . . . also . . . in cases where an unfortunate collocation of words produces an obscene suggestion.

Puttenham (253f)
Scheme. When our speech may be drawn to a reprobate sense. . . . Tolerable . . . chiefly to the intent to move laughter and to make sport or to give it some pretty strange grace. . . . Vice. Such words as may be drawn to a foul and unshamefast sense which our courtly maker shall in any case shun. . . . Another sort of illfavoured speech subject to this vice, . . . is in the manner of illshapen sound and accent [see under CACOPHONIA].

EXAMPLES
Puttenham (254)

> Jape with me but hurt me not,
> Board with me but shame me not.

Sentenia (Gnome)
also known as *indicatio*

Quintilian (VIII, v)
The epigram, striking reflections such as are more specially introduced at the close of periods. . . . Forms: *aphorisms* . . . resemble the decrees or resolutions of public bodies. . . . At times it is simple while at other times a reason for the statement may be added. Sometimes it may be double. *Enthymeme* [see under CONTRARIUM], *epiphonema* [see under ACCLAMATIO], *noema* [see under INTIMITATIO], *clausula* . . . a conclusion, the unexpected [see under IMPROVISUM]. Other *sententiae* depend upon allusion, . . . others are transferred from one context to another, . . . others are produced by the doubling of a phrase, . . . others by a comparison.
Bad *sententiae* depend only upon a play of words, . . . a false comparison, . . . or absurdities of wit.

Erasmus (8of)
For plenitude of thought. A kind of *exemplum*. These may be scattered throughout all parts of the speech. . . . They may be universal, personal, . . . simple or double, . . . direct or figurative, . . . commonplace or with the meaning partly concealed.

Susenbrotus (94f)
Scheme. A brief statement of an important maxim inserted into a speech. It may be like an *emblem* or an *apophthegm* and it gives to the speech authority and dignity.

Puttenham (235)
Scheme. For weighty causes and great purposes . . . advice or counsel. A manner of speech to allege texts or authorities of witty sentence such as match moral doctrine and teach wisdom and good behaviour.

EXAMPLES
Peacham (189)
As evil gotten goods are evil spent.
Necessity hath no law.
Flattery getteth friendship, and truth hatred.

Hoskins (39)
Man's experience is woman's best eyesight.
He felt, valuing money higher than equity, that guiltiness is not always with ease oppressed (with *meiosis, not always with ease* for *ever* and *hardly*).
Who stands only upon defence stands upon no defence (with *syneciosis* and *epanodos*).

Ad Herennium, Cicero, Fortunatianus
Melancthon, Sherry, Scaliger, Day

Series (Irmos)
also known as *tractum, nexum*

Susenbrotus (38f)
Scheme. When a passage consists of a continued speech, a series, uniformly listed in the same case from the beginning of the series to the end.

Peacham (1577, Hi)
Scheme. When an unfashioned order of speech is long continued, and
... stretched out to the end, still after one sort, void of all round and
sweet composition.

Puttenham (176)
A manner of speech drawn out at length and going all after one tenor
with an imperfect sense till you come to the last word or verse which
concludes the whole premises with a perfect sense and full period.

EXAMPLES

Peacham (Hi)
Harken all you that love justice, and would have reason bear rule, in all
controversies and debates, knowing how all men might to the utter-
most of their power, not having regard to men, maintain the same . . .
against all such as would . . . bring in all manner of disorders among
good men, that do daily wish to live in peace, . . . wherein debates do
daily grow and increase to a huge heap.

Puttenham (176)
In the song of Petrarch translated by Wyatt, *If weaker care . . . , then I
do love again* finishes the song with a full and perfect sense.

Day

Sermocinatio (Dialogismos)

Ad Herennium (IV, 65)
Whenever in a speech we attribute to some person direct speech which
as set forth conforms with his character.

Erasmus (33)
The attribution to an individual of language in harmony with his age,
birth, country, life, spirit, and behaviour. This figure is found in histories, but is more common in the poets.

Scaliger (III, xxv)
Under *tractatio*. When a particular direct speech is attributed to a character, . . . a means of portraying this character.

Peacham (137)
Scheme. The orator feigneth a person and maketh him speak . . . when the person whom the orator feigneth speaketh all himself, then it is *prosopopoeia*, but when the orator answereth now and then to the question, which the feigned person objecteth to him, it is called *sermocinatio*.

EXAMPLE

Peacham (137f)
Ephraim thinketh thus: . . . I am rich, I have goods enough, in all my works shall not one fault be found that I have offended: be it so, yet I am the Lord thy God which brought thee from the land of Egypt, and yet will I make thee dwell in tabernacles, as in the days of the solemn feast.

Quintilian
Melancthon, Sherry, Puttenham, Day

Similiter cadens (Omoeoptoton)

Quintilian (IX, iii, 78)
Scheme. Correspondence between clauses is produced by the use of similar cases. . . . This does not necessarily involve identity in termination since it means no more than similarity of case . . . and does not always occur at the end of a sentence.

Wilson (202)
Scheme. Sentences also are said to fall like when diverse words in one sentence end in like cases, and that in rhyme.

Peacham (53f)
Scheme. A figure which endeth diverse clauses with like cases, but in respect of the English tongue which is not varied by cases, we may call it setting of diverse nouns in one sentence which end alike with the same letter or syllable . . . to delight the ear by the like fall and similitude of the sound, wherein the nature of that sense takes singular pleasure.

169

EXAMPLES

Wilson (202)
By great travail is gotten much avail, by earnest affection men learn discretion.

Peacham (54)
He came into Sicilia, and then spied out Africa: and after that came with his army into Sardinia.
In activity commendable, in a commonwealth profitable, and in war terrible.

Ad Herennium, Cicero, Aquila
Trapezuntius, Melancthon, Susenbrotus, Sherry, Scaliger, Day

Similiter desinens (Omoeoteleuton)

Quintilian (IX, iii, 77)
Scheme. When clauses conclude alike, the same syllables being placed at the end of each . . . in the ending of two or more sentences.

Susenbrotus (55)
Scheme. When words or sentences have similar endings.

Wilson (202)
Scheme. The sentences are said to end like, when those words do end in like syllables which do lack cases.

Puttenham (173)
Tunable and melodious . . . the Greeks used a manner of speech . . . in their proses that went by clauses finishing in words of like tune and might be by using like cases, tenses and other points of consonance, . . . the nearest approach to our vulgar rhyme.

EXAMPLES

Wilson (202)
Thou lives wickedly, thou speakest naughtily.

Puttenham (173)
>   Weeping creeping beseeching I won
>   The love at length of Lady Lucian.
>
>   For such mishaps as be remediless,
>   To sorrow for them it is but foolishness.

Peacham (54)
He is esteemed eloquent which can invent wittily, remember perfectly, dispose orderly, figure diversely, pronounce aptly, confirm strongly, and conclude directly.

Ad Herennium, Cicero, Aquila
Trapezuntius, Melancthon, Sherry, Scaliger, Day

Similitudo (Omoeosis)

Quintilian (VIII, iii, 72ff)
The invention of *similitudines* has provided an admirable means of illuminating our description. Some . . . are for insertion among our arguments to help our proof while others . . . make our pictures yet more vivid. . . . Anything that is selected for the purpose of illuminating something else must itself be clearer than that which it is to illustrate. . . . The simile as an ornament serves to make oratory sublime, rich or striking, . . . the commonplace . . . to create an impression of sincerity.

Melancthon (*De Rhetorica*, Cii^v)
Trope. The forms of similitude are *paradigma* (*exemplum*), *apologia* (*fabella*) and *parabola*.

Susenbrotus (99f)
Scheme. When something similar (from a different context) is applied to some situation, or when one thing is compared to another in respect of similarity. . . . It also occurs when, using the similarity of something known, we branch out into a discussion of something unknown.

Hoskins (10)
A *similitude* hath two sentences, of several proper terms compared. . . . It is the ground of all emblems, allegories, fables and fictions.

EXAMPLES

Peacham (159f)

Even as the light of a candle is opprest with the brightness of the sun, so the estimation of corporal things must needs be darkened, drowned, and destroyed by the glory and greatness of virtue.

As in dangerous sailing the helm is not committed to him that is richest or noblest of birth, but to him that hath the best knowledge in guiding the ship: even so is it requisite not to give the principality of government to him that is of more wealth than others, or of nobler blood, but to him that excelleth other men in wisdom and loyalty.

Hoskins (10)

Even as a castle compassed about with rivers cannot be battered or undermined, Philoclea, defended round about with virtuous resolutions, could neither be forced nor surprised by deceit.

Ad Herennium, Cicero, Rufinianus
Wilson, Puttenham, Day

Subintellectio (Synecdoche)

also known as *intellectio*

Quintilian (VIII, vi, 19)

Trope. The power to give variety to our language by making us realise many things from one, the whole from a part, the genus from a species, things which follow from things which have preceded; or the whole process may be reversed. . . . A figure more freely employed by poets than orators.

Erasmus (33)

For plenitude of words. When we understand one thing for another, . . . the whole for the part, . . . the species for the genus. . . . any way in which one thing is understood from another.

Fraunce (21ff)

Trope. *Synecdoche* of the part is, when by a part we mean the whole and it is either of the member, when by one integral member the whole is signified, or of the special . . . when by the special we note the general. . . . Of the whole is when by the whole we mean a part, either of the integral whole or general and universal. Of the integral when by the whole integral we mean a part. . . . Of the general is when by the general we intend the special, so the plural for the singular, so the Poet for Virgil.

Puttenham (185)
A word . . . by which we drive the hearer to conceive more or less beyond or otherwise than the letter expresseth . . . and generally one thing out of another by manner of contrariety to the word which is spoken.

EXAMPLES

Fraunce (22)
Basilius having combed and tricked himself more curiously, than any times forty winters before.

Fraunce (23)
Neither he shews reverence to a Prince, nor mercy to a beggar.

Hoskins (11)
Ay, my name is tossed and censured by many tongues.
He carries a goldsmith's shop on his fingers.
Put up your weapon (for *your dagger*).
The Spaniard, they say, comes against us.

Ad Herennium
Melancthon, Susenbrotus, Talaeus, Sherry, Wilson, Day, Puttenham

Subjectio (Hypophora)
also known as *occupatio* (not to be confused with *paralepsis*)

Ad Herennium (IV, 33)
When we enquire of our adversaries or ask ourselves what they may say in their favour or against us and then we subjoin what ought or ought not to be said that will be favourable to us or prejudicial to the opposition.

Talaeus (103f)
Scheme. When we discuss the objections which may be made against our case and reply to these ourselves, . . . often using the form of *prosopopoeia* . . . to present the opposing argument as the direct speech of the opponent.

EXAMPLE

Ad Herennium (IV, 33)
From what source has the defendant become so wealthy? Has an ample patrimony been left to him? But his father's goods were sold. Has some bequest come to him? That cannot be urged: on the contrary he has even been disinherited by all his kin.

Quintilian
Erasmus, Melancthon

Subjunctio (Epizeuxis)
also known as *adjectio*

Quintilian (IX, iii, 28)
Scheme. Words may be doubled with a view to amplification . . . or to excite pity . . . or ironically, to disparage.

Susenbrotus (50)
Scheme. When we repeat a word unnaturally in the full flow of utterance for the sake of greater vehemence.

Talaeus (55)
Scheme. When the same sound is immediately repeated in the same sentence.

Peacham (47)
Scheme. A word is repeated, for the greater vehemency, and nothing put between. . . . This figure may also be joined with other repetition.

Hoskins (12)
A repetition of the same word or sound immediately or without interposition of any other.

174

EXAMPLES

Peacham (41)
O Coridon, Coridon what madness hath thee moved?
O my son Absolom, my son, my son Absolom, would God I had died
for thee, O Absolom my son my son.

Hoskins (12)
O let not, let not from you be poured upon me destruction.
Tormented? Tormented? torment of my soul, Philoclea, tormented?

Aquila
Wilson, Puttenham, Day

Submutatio (Hypallage)
(not to be confused with *metonymia*)

Susenbrotus (34)
Scheme. A passage in which things are presented in inverse order.

Peacham (1577, Gi)
Scheme. When a sentence is said with a contrary order of words.

Puttenham (171)
A working by exchange: changing the true construction and application of the words whereby the sense is perverted and made very
absurd.

Day (83)
When by change of property in application a thing is delivered.

EXAMPLES

Peacham (Gi)
Open the day, and see if it be the window.
I would make no more ado, but take a door and break open the axe.

Puttenham (171)
Stay with me and dine not (for *dine with me and stay not*).

Melancthon, Day

175

Tempus (Cronographia)

Erasmus (55)
The description of time ... Sometimes ... employed simply for the sake of giving pleasure. .... Descriptions of the seasons, holidays, special occasions and so on.

Puttenham (239)
Scheme. If we describe the time or season of the year, ... we call such description the counterfeit time.

Peacham (142)
Scheme. When the orator describeth any time for delectations sake, as the morning, the evening, midnight ... the spring ... the time of war, the time of peace, the old time.

EXAMPLES

Peacham (142)
The time when darkness ariseth in the East, and stars begin to appear, when labourers forsake the fields, birds betake themselves to their night boughs, and beasts to their harbour, and when the silence of all creatures is increased through desire of rest.
It was night, and all weary creatures took their sweet slumber, both woods and raging seas had left their sounds, and stars now hiding in the midst of the night, when every field is hushed.

Quintilian
Melancthon, Susenbrotus, Sherry, Scaliger

Testamentum (Diatyposis)
(not to be confused with *tractatio*) also known as *informatio*

Peacham (92)
Scheme. The orator commendeth certain profitable rules and precepts to his hearers and to posterity.

EXAMPLES

Peacham (92)

My son hearken unto my wisdom, and incline thine ear unto my pru-
dence, that thou maist regard counsel, and thy lips observe knowledge.
My son keep thy fathers commandments, and forsake not the law of
thy mother.

Testatio (Martyria)

Peacham (85f)

Scheme. The orator confirmeth something by his own experience . . .
speaketh of things removed from the knowledge of his hearers, and
allegeth his own testimony, grounded upon his own knowledge . . .
joined with delectation, for by nature men take more pleasure to hear
the author of experience speak himself.

EXAMPLES

Peacham (85)

I have seen the foolish deep rooted and suddenly I cursed his habitation.
That which was from the beginning, which we have heard, which we
have seen with our eyes, which we have looked upon.
The traveller maketh descriptions of cities and countries, where he hath
been, and declareth the sundry fashions and strange manners of far
nations and people.

Quintilian

Tolerantia (Apocarteresis)

Robortellus (49)

From Demetrius. When we relinquish all hope.

Peacham (83f)

Scheme. The speaker signifieth that he calleth away all hope concerning something and turneth it another way.

EXAMPLES

Peacham (83)
He hath destroyed me on every side, and I am gone, and he hath removed mine hope like a tree.

Peacham (84)
Let the widow weep, and the fatherless children lament: Let kinsfolk sorrow and friends mourn, yet cannot all this prevail for he is gone and cannot be called again . . . and therefore think on men that live and let the dead rest.

Tractatio (Diatyposis)
also known as *descriptio, deformatio*

Quintilian (IX, ii, 41)
Vivid description.

Scaliger (III, xxxiii)
A generic term for that group of figures which describes things as they are, putting their features before the eyes of the hearer and illuminating each detail.

EXAMPLE

Quintilian (IX, ii, 41)
Though you cannot see this with your bodily eyes you can see it with the mind's eye.

Aquila, Fortunatianus

Traductio

Quintilian (IX, iii, 71f)
The transference of the meaning from one word to another . . . employed to distinguish the exact meanings of things as in 'This curse to the state could be repressed for a time, but not suppressed for ever' . . . or with both a figurative form and excellent sense, *emit morte immortalitem* [see also ALLUSIO].

Puttenham (203f)
Scheme. When you turn and tranlace a word into many sundry shapes as the tailor doth his garment and after that sort do play with him in your ditty.

Peacham (49)
Scheme. A form of speech which repeateth one word often times in one sentence, making the oration more pleasant to the ear. . . . This exornation is compared to pleasant repetitions and divisions in music.

EXAMPLES

Puttenham (204)
>   Who lives in love his life is full of fears,
>   To lose his love, livelihood or liberty
>   But lively sprites that young and reckless be,
>   Think that there is no living like to theirs.

Peacham (49)
O king thou art a king of kings.
In the beginning was the word, and the word was with God, and God was the word.

Cicero
Wilson

Transgressio (Hyperbaton)
also know as *perversio*

Quintilian (VIII, vi, 62f)
Trope. The transposition of a word . . . to some distance from its original place in order to secure an ornamental effect . . . often demanded by the structure of the sentence and the claims of elegance. It is impossible to make our prose rhythmical without it. . . . There is reason for calling such a transposition a trope since the meaning is not complete until the two words have been put together.

Susenbrotus (31)
Scheme. A change or mutation of the normally correct order of either words or phrases, . . . used when no other means will make the passage rythmical.

Talaeus (44)
Scheme. An upsetting of normal word order, carried on at some length.

Peacham (1577, Fiiiᵛ)
Scheme. When the right and lawful order of words or clauses, is altered by unproper placing, or . . . when words or clauses be transposed from the plain order of construction, to make the oration more lofty.

Puttenham (168)
A working by disorder. . . . The Greek name for all the auricular figures of disorder, such as *parenthesis, hysteron proteron* etc.

EXAMPLE
Peacham (Fiiiᵛ)
What heart can of the Greeks or soldiers, one of all Ulisses' rout refrain to weep.

Ad Herennium
Trapezuntius, Melancthon, Sherry, Scaliger

Transitio (Metabasis)
also known as *sejunctio*

Ad Herennium (IV, 35)
When what has been said is briefly recalled and we briefly propound what is to follow. . . . This gives emphasis to our argument and makes it more memorable.

Wilson (182)
Scheme. When we go from one matter to another, we use this kind of phrase.

180

Scaliger (III, lxxvi)
Under *hyperbole*. This figure adds nothing to the meaning but simply repeats what has been said and introduces what will be said, . . . using examples . . . or invocations.

Peacham (175)
Scheme. The orator in a few words showeth what hath been already said, and also what shall be said next, and that diverse ways. From the equal, . . . the unequal, . . . the like, . . . the contrary, . . . by prevention of occupations, . . . by reprehension, . . . from consequents.

EXAMPLES

Wilson (182)
I have told you the cause of all this evil, now I will tell you a remedy for the same.

Peacham (175)
(From the like) I have hitherto made mention of his noble enterprises in France, and now I rehearse his worthy acts done near to Rome.
(By prevention or occupation) Peradventure you think me long in the threatenings of the law, I will now pass to the sweet promises of the Gospel.
(From consequents) You have been told how he promised, and now I will tell you how he performed.

*Cicero, Rutilius Lupus, Quintilian, Rufinianus, Fortunatianus
Melancthon, Susenbrotus, Sherry, Day*

Translatio (Metaphora)

Ad Herennium (IV, 45)
When a word is transferred from one thing to another . . . a means of presenting our subject as if before the eyes of the audience, of attaining brevity, avoiding obscenity, of amplification and ornament.

Quintilian (VIII, vi, 4ff)
Trope. The commonest and by far the most beautiful of tropes. . . . For if it be correctly and appropriately applied it is quite impossible for its

effect to be commonplace, mean or unpleasing. It adds to the copiousness of language by the interchange of words and by borrowing and
succeeds in the supremely difficult task of providing a name for everything. A noun or verb is transferred from the place to which it properly
belongs to another where there is no literal term or the transferred is
better than the literal. . . . Metaphor is a shorter form of *similitudo* . . .
in the latter we compare some object to the thing which we wish to
describe whereas in the former this object is actually substituted for the
thing. . . . Metaphor falls into four classes . . . one living thing is substituted for another, . . . inanimate things for inanimate, or inanimate
for animate . . . or animate for inanimate . . . if we introduce metaphors
in one continuous series our language will become allegorical and
enigmatic.

Erasmus (28f)
For plenitude of words. We substitute for a word a word whose meaning is very close to the original word . . . We call a metaphor *acoloutha*,
when the substitution is reciprocal, as in 'pilot' for 'charioteer', and
anacoloutha when it is non-reciprocal. We can call a 'summit' a 'crown'
but not vice versa. . . . Sometimes, to a metaphor we may add an
explanation.

Susenbrotus (6)
Trope. When we transfer a word from its proper meaning to another
but related meaning . . . for the purposes of clarity, perspicuity and
grace, . . . for emphasis . . . or ornament.

Scaliger (III, l)
Under *tractatio*. When we transpose the meaning of the same word from
one concept to another.

Fraunce (15)
Trope. When the like is signified by the like: so then a metaphor is
nothing but a similitude contracted into one word. There is no trope
more flourishing than a metaphor, especially if it be applied to the
senses, and among these chiefly to the eye, which is the quickest of all
the senses.

182

Hoskins (8)

The borrowing of one word to express a thing with more light and better note, though not so directly and properly as the natural name of the thing meant would signify. . . . And though all metaphors go beyond the signification of things, yet are they requisite to match the compassing sweetness of men's minds, that are not content to fix themselves upon one thing but they must wander into the confines. . . . Besides, a metaphor is pleasant because it enricheth our knowledge with two things at once, with the truth and with similitude.

EXAMPLES

Wilson (172f)

Ah sirra, I am glad I have smelled you out.

Fraunce (16)

Alas the race
Of all my thoughts, hath neither stop, nor start,
But only *Stella*'s eyes and *Stella*'s heart.

Began to throw her thoughts into each corner of her invention.

Fraunce (17)

She gave him the wooden salutation you heard of.

Peacham (5)

Hear no counsel against innocent blood (that is, *consent not to that counsel*).

Peacham (7)

And having once tasted of the heavenly gifts (*experienced*).

Hoskins (8)

Swords hungry of blood.

Heads disinherited of their natural signories (whereby we understand both beheading and the government of the head over the body).

To divorce the fair marriage of the head and the body.

Cicero, Fortunatianus
Melancthon, Talaeus, Sherry, Puttenham, Day

Transmissio (Metastasis)
also known as *transmotio*

Puttenham (233)
Scheme. To flit from one matter to another, as a thing meet to be forsaken and another entered upon.

Peacham (181)
Scheme. A form of speech by which we turn back those things that are objected against us to them which laid them to us.

EXAMPLE

Peacham (181)
When Antony charged Cicero that he was the cause of civil war raised between Pompeius and Caesar, Cicero rebounded the same accusation to Antony, saying: Thou Marcus Antony, thou I say gavest to Caesar (willing to turn all upside down) cause to make war against thy country. It is not I that trouble Israel, but thou and thy father's house.

Melancthon

Transmutatio (Metonymia)
also known as *hypallage* (not to be confused with *submutatio*), *transnominatio*, *denominatio*

Quintilian (VIII, vi, 23ff)
Trope. The substitution of one name for another. . . . To indicate an invention by substituting the name of the inventor or a possession by substituting the name of the possessor . . . or vice versa.

Erasmus (32)
For plenitude of words. The change of name. . . . To this class should be referred those terms used alike of men and things, such as 'eloquent'.

Susenbrotus (7f)
Trope. A noun is substituted for a noun in such a way that we substitute the cause of the thing of which we are speaking for the thing itself. . . .

We do this in several ways, substituting the inventor for his invention, . . . the container for the thing contained or vice versa, . . . an author for his work, . . . the sign for the thing signified.

Fraunce (4ff)
Trope. Useth the name of one thing for the name of another that agreeth with it. . . . The *metonymia* of the cause is double, of the efficient cause as when we put the author and inventor for the things by him invented . . . of the thing caused, when we attribute that to the efficient which is made by the efficient . . . of the subject, when the word that properly signifieth the subject is brought to express the thing adjoined thereunto, as when the thing that containeth is put for that which is contained . . . of the adjunct when by the adjunct we express the subject. So the names of virtues and vices are used for virtuous or vicious men.

EXAMPLES

Wilson (175)
Put upon thou the Lord Jesus Christ.
The Pope is banished England.

Fraunce (5)
(Of the cause)
   Therefore, alas, you use vile Vulcan's spite
   Which nothing spares, to melt that virgin's wax.
(Of the thing caused)
    Nay even cold death inflamed with hot desire
    Her to enjoy where joy itself is thrall.
(Of the subject)
  Here do ye find in truth this strange operation of Love,
  How to the wood love runs, as well as rides to the palace.
(Of the adjunct) Howsoever it be, my death shall triumph over thy cruelty.

Hoskins (10)
I want silver (meaning *money*).
The city met the Queen (for *the citizens*).

Ad Herennium, Cicero
Melancthon, Talaeus, Puttenham, Day, Peacham

Transumptio (Metalepsis)

Quintilian (VIII, vi, 37)
Trope. Provides a transition from one trope to another. . . . It is in the nature of *metalepsis* to form a kind of intermediate step between the term transferred and the thing to which it is transferred, having no meaning in itself but merely providing a transition. . . . I see no use in it except in comedy.

Erasmus (31f)
For plenitude of words. Similar to *abusio*, when we proceed by steps to that we wish to express, as in 'sharp' for 'swift'. It is used more often in verse than in prose.

Wilson (175)
Trope. When by degrees we go to that, which is to be showed.

Peacham (23f)
Trope. The orator in one word expressed, signifieth another word or thing removed from it by certain degrees . . . a kind of *metonymia* signifying a cause far off by an effect nigh at hand . . . seldom used. . . . It teacheth the understanding to dive down to the bottom of the sense.

EXAMPLES

Wilson (175)
Such a one lieth in a dark dungeon (now in speaking of darkness we understand closeness, by closeness we gather blackness, and by blackness we judge deepness).

Puttenham (183)
> Woe worth the mountain that the mast bear
> Which was the first causer of all my care.

(Medea cursing Jason)

Peacham (23)
Virgil by ears of corn signifieth summers, and by summers, years.

Peacham (24)
The tongues of sucking children do cleave to the roof of their mouths
for very thirst (the Prophet signifieth the dry breasts of the mothers
and by the dry breasts the extreme famine of the people).

Melancthon, Susenbrotus, Sherry, Day

Tropus

Quintilian (VIII, vi, 1ff)
The generic term for a group of figures. By a trope is meant the artistic
alteration of a word or phrase from its proper meaning to another. . . .
There are two kinds: those involving change of meaning and those
which are employed in the oration for ornament and amplification but
do not necessarily change the meaning.

Talaeus (3ff)
When a word is altered from its original meaning to another. . . . This
can be a source of ambiguity and obscurity. There are two basic kinds,
metonymia and *ironia*.

Fraunce (3f)
When a word is turned from his natural signification to some other so
conveniently, as that it seem rather willingly led, than driven by force
to that other signification. . . . There be two kinds of tropes. The first
containeth *metonymia*, the change of name: and *ironia*, a scoffing or
jesting speech: the second comprehendeth a *metaphor* and *synecdoche*.

Turpiloquum (Aeschrologia)
(see also SCURRA)

Veltkirchius (10)
Vice. When one does not abstain from using the proper term for something disgusting.

Sherry (Ci^v)
Vice. *Turpis loquutio*, when the words be spoken or joined together, that they may be wrung into a filthy sense.

EXAMPLE
Sherry (Ci^v)
Of this it needeth not to put any example when lewd persons will soon find enough.

Urbanitas (Asteismus)
also known as *facetia*

Susenbrotus (15)
Trope. A kind of little game relying on things unexpected or absurd. The urbane joke or game has nothing in it of rustic simplicity: it is a civilised form of jest.

Puttenham (190)
When we speak by a manner of pleasantry or merry scoff, that is, by a kind of mock whereof the sense is far fetched and without any gall or offence.

Peacham (33f)
Trope. A witty jesting in civil manner, and gracing of speech with some merry conceit ... any mirth or pleasant speech which is void of rustical simplicity and rudeness ... taken from diverse places but chiefly from *equivocation*, as when a word having two significations, is expressed in the one, and understood in the other, either contrary, or at least much differing ... most witty, ... or from fallacy, ... when a saying is captiously taken, and turned to another sense, contrary or much differing from the meaning of the speaker, ... or from pleasant imitations of men's speech and fashions, ... reports of merry actions and accidents.

EXAMPLES
Peacham (34)
To one demanding of Diogenes what he would take for a knock on his pate, he made this answer, that he would take a helmet.

To one that said he knew not if he should be put out of his house where to hide his head: another made him answer, that he might hide it in his cap.

Quintilian, Rufinianus
Sherry, Day

The Figures: Greek Names Only

Adynaton

Melancthon (Elementorum, 44f)
Scheme. A kind of paradox, [the figure by which we admit that our
message is beyond the power of words to convey.]

EXAMPLE

Melancthon (44f)
Words cannot convey how much your letters have delighted me.

Fortunatianus

Aenos

Scaliger (III, lxxxiv)
Under *allegory*. Generally the narrating of events worthy of praise and
admiration. . . . It is concerned with what is serious. Moreover, it
describes that which because of its obscurity is noticed only by the wise.

Sherry (Fvii)
Scheme. A saying or a sentence taken out of a tale.

EXAMPLE

Sherry (Fvii)
The interpretations of fables and their allegories.

Quintilian

Alloeosis

Quintilian (IX, iii, 92)
Scheme. Mutation of the kind which Rutilius calls *alloeosis* . . . to point
out the differences between men, things and deeds: if it is used on an
extended scale it is not a figure, if on a narrower scale it is mere
antitheton.

Scaliger (IV, xxxvi)
Scheme. When we change the gender of a word or the case of a noun.

EXAMPLES

Scaliger (IV, xxxvi)
Fabricor (*pro fabrico*)
Ulyssi (*pro Ulyssis*)

Rutilius Lupus

Allotheta
also known as *alloeosis*

Susenbrotus (42f)
Scheme. When we change the number, tense, gender, person or mood
of a word.

Peacham (1577, Hiii)
Scheme. When we put one case for another, one gender for another
gender, number for number, mood for mood, tense for tense, and
person for person, whose kinds be these that follow: *enallage, endiadis,
anthimeria*.

EXAMPLES

Susenbrotus (42f)

Adeon homines immutarier ex amore, ut non cognoscas eundem esse (pro eosdem).

Interea servitia repudiabat, cuius rei initio ad eum magnae copiae concurrebant (pro quorum).

Anapodoton

Peacham (1577, Fiᵛ)

Scheme. An oration wanting one member, or when in a sentence there is some little clause left out, either in the beginning, midst, or end.

EXAMPLES

Peacham (Fiᵛ)

Which if he do refuse, he shall be defied, but if he do accept them . . . (so leaving of the other part unsaid).

Peacham (Fii)

If you do as I have counselled you, and be ruled by your friends, they will do for you. If not, well, I will say no more.

Anoiconometon

Quintilian (VIII, iii, 59)

Vice. Faulty arrangement.

Veltkirchius, Robortellus

Antanaclasis

Quintilian (IX, iii, 68)

Scheme. The same word is used in two different meanings. . . . Sometimes such difference in meaning is obtained not by using the same word, but one like it.

Susenbrotus (56)
Scheme. Use of the one word with two contrary meanings . . . more often found in games and jokes.

Puttenham (207)
Scheme. The scheme playeth with one word written all alike but carrying diverse senses.

Peacham (56f)
Scheme. A figure which repeateth a word that hath two significations and the one of them contrary, or at least unlike the other.

EXAMPLES

Peacham (56)
Care for those things which may discharge you of all care.

Peacham (57)
In thy youth learn some craft, that in thy age thou mayst get thy living without craft.

Melancthon, Day

Antapodosis

Quintilian (VIII, iii, 77f)
A type of simile which places both subjects of a comparison before our very eyes, displaying them side by side.

Scaliger (III, li)
A kind of *comparatio*. The reasoning which adjusts both sides of a comparison to each other. . . . It includes a form of speech added to previous forms, such as *retributio* joined to *propositio*.

EXAMPLE

Quintilian (VIII, iii, 80)
For as tempests are generally preceded by some premonitory signs in the heaven, but often, on the other hand, break forth for some obscure reason without any warning whatsoever, so in the tempests which sway

the people at our Roman elections we are not seldom in a position to discern their origin, and yet, it is frequently so obscure that the storm seems to have burst without any apparent cause.

Anthimeria

Peacham (Hiv^v)
Scheme. A kind of *allotheta*. When we put one part of speech for another . . . an adverb for a noun . . . a noun for an adverb.

EXAMPLES
Peacham (Hiv^v)
So was all his life (for *such was all his life*).
He spake very hot you all can tell (for *he spoke very hotly*).

Antirresis

Quintilian (IX, ii, 106)
Scheme. Refutation.

Peacham (88f)
Scheme. A form of speech by which the orator rejecteth the authority, opinion or sentence of some person: for the error or wickedness in it.

EXAMPLES
Peacham (89)
Thou speakest like a foolish woman.
Be not deceived, evil words corrupt good manners.

Rutilius Lupus

Apoplanesis

Rufinianus (58)
Scheme. When some point against us has come before the judge or has been moved by the adversary, we obscure it by promising to speak of

it in its place, raise another matter and move on to other things, drawing the attention of the judge from the point against us.

Peacham (117)
Scheme. A kind of aversion or turning away, and it is when the speaker leadeth away the mind of his hearer, from the matter propounded or question in hand, which maketh much against him.

EXAMPLE
Peacham (117)
Cicero when he should have answered to an accusation . . . that Caelius poisoned Metellus . . . he digressed by and by to Metellus' death and maketh a suspicion that he was poisoned by . . . Clodius: he sigheth, weepeth, and bewaileth that death whereby he staieth and appeaseth his adversaries, and causeth them to mourn with him.

Astrothesia

Sherry (Eiii)
Scheme. The description of stars.

Barbarismos

Ad Herennium (IV, 17)
Vice of style. It occurs if the verbal expression is incorrect.

Puttenham (250)
Vice of style. When any strange word not of the natural Greek or Latin was spoken . . . or when any of their own natural words were sounded and pronounced with strange and illshapen accents or written by wrong orthography.

EXAMPLE
Puttenham (250)
A dousand (for *a thousand*)

Quintilian
Veltkirchius, Sherry

Bomphiologia

Sherry (Dvii)
Scheme. *Verborum bombus*. When small and trifling things are set out
with great gazing words.

Puttenham (259f)
Vice. Such bombasted words as seem altogether forced full of wind,
being a great deal too high and lofty for the matter.

EXAMPLE
Sherry (Dvii)
Terence's boasting soldier.

Brachiepeia

Peacham (182)

Scheme. A form of speech by which the matter is briefly told with no
more words than those that be necessary: or when the orator by
brevity cutteth off the expectation of the hearers.

EXAMPLES
Peacham (182)
Pompeius prepared for war in winter, began it in spring and finished
it in summer.
The corpse goeth before, we follow after, we come to the grave, it is
put into the fire, a lamentation is made.

Cacophonia
also known as *cacemphaton* (not to be confused with *scurra*)

Veltkirchius (10)
Vice. Something that sounds bad.

Susenbrotus (36)
Vice. A disagreeable and inharmonious composition of sounds as, for example, too much alliteration.

Peacham (50)
Vice. A harsh and jarring sound.

EXAMPLE
Peacham (50)
Neither honour, nor nobility.
> In my drowsy and dreadful dream, me thought
> I saw a Dragon drinking blood.

Cacosyntheton

Quintilian (VIII, iii, 59)
Vice. The faulty collocation of words.

Peacham (1577, Giv)
Vice. When good words be ill applied or placed, called a deformed composition . . . or sometime when they be ill placed.

Puttenham (253)
Vice. Ill disposition or placing of your words in a clause or sentence.

EXAMPLE
Peacham (Giv)
There is small adversity between your mare and mine.
A foolish fellow when I saw before the King, stand laughing.

Sherry

Charientismos

Susenbrotus (16)
Trope. When with softer words we appease a harsh criticism, or we soften harsh facts with gracious words.

Puttenham (191)
We give a mock under smooth and lowly words . . . a mild and appeasing mockery.

Peacham (36)
Trope. A form of speech which mitigateth hard matters with pleasant words.

EXAMPLES

Puttenham (191)
He that heard one . . . say, thou art sure to be hanged ere thou die: quoth the other very soberly. Sir I know your mastership speaks but in jest.

Peacham (36)
Had not the wine failed we had spoken much worse (by which a man accused of slander meant that the words proceeded rather from wine than malice).

Quintilian, Rufinianus
Sherry, Day

Chiasmos

Scaliger (IV, xxxviii)
Scheme. When the first element and the fourth, and the second and the third are conjoined giving a scissor formation in the sentence.

Trapezuntius

Emblem

Hoskins (9f)
An *emblem* is but one part of the similitude, the other part (viz., the application) expressed indifferently and jointly in one sentence, with words some proper to the one part, some to the other.

o   199

EXAMPLE

Hoskins (10)

Plant (depict) a castle compassed with rivers and let the word be
neither by siege nor undermining: this is an emblem, the proper terms of
the one part . . . *Philoclea's* virtue; *environed, rivers, battered, undermined,*
the terms of the other part (the emblem).

Puttenham

Emphasis

Quintilian (VIII, iii, 83)

A virtue of style. *Emphasis* succeeds in revealing a deeper meaning than
is actually expressed by the words. There are two kinds: the one means
more than it says, the other often means something which it does not
actually say . . . and consists either in the complete suppression of a
word or in the deliberate omission to utter it.

Quintilian (IX, ii, 64)

Scheme. When some hidden meaning is extracted from some phrase,
as in the following passage from Virgil:

> Might not I have lived,
> From wedlock free, a life without a strain,
> Happy as beasts are happy?

For, although Dido complains of marriage, yet her passionate out-
burst shows that she regards life without wedlock as no life for a man,
but for the beasts of the field.

Susenbrotus (44f)

Scheme. By this figure we understand something greater and of more
significance than the word itself declares . . . or more is meant than is
said . . . or something is meant which is not said.

Scaliger (III, lxxix)

Under *eclipsis.* When more is understood than is said.

Puttenham (184)
One notable mean to affect the mind is to enforce the sense of any thing by a word of more than ordinary efficacy and nevertheless is not apparent but . . . secretly implied.

Peacham (178)
Scheme. A form of speech which signifieth that which it does not express, the signification whereof is understood either by the manner of the pronunciation, or by the nature of the words themselves.

EXAMPLES

Puttenham (184)
O sin itself, not wretch but wretchedness (of a very evil man).

Peacham (178)
Wilt thou believe a Cretan?
I will say to corruption thou art my father, and to the worm thou art my mother and my sister.

Endiadis

Susenbrotus (35)
Scheme. To divide a single thing into two by placing a conjunction in the middle—for the sake of the poetry.

Peacham (1577, Hivf)
Scheme. When a substantive is put for an adjective of the same signification.

Puttenham (177)
To make two of one not thereunto constrained.

EXAMPLES

Peacham (Hivf)
He is a man of great wisdom (for *He is a very wise man*).
A man of great wealth (for *a wealthy man*).

Puttenham (177)
Your lowers nor your looks (for *your lowering looks*).
Of fortune nor her frowning face (for *fortune's frowning face*).

Day

Enigma

Quintilian (VIII, vi, 52f)
Trope. A kind of allegory. When . . . an allegory is too obscure we call
it a riddle: such riddles are . . . to be regarded as blemishes in view of
the fact that lucidity is a virtue; nevertheless they are used by poets.

Susenbrotus (13)
Trope. It is an obscure allegory in which you can conceal hidden
meanings for words. It is distinguished from allegory proper whose
meaning is evident, clear and manifest.

Scaliger (III, lxxxiv)
An obscure passage which arrives at a known fact indirectly, . . .
ridiculous or jocose or not without learning.

Peacham (27f)
Trope. It differs from allegory in obscurity . . . a sentence or form of
speech, which for the darkness, the sense may hardly be gathered. . . .
More convenient to poets, . . . to high and heavenly visions, than to the
form of familiar and proper speech.

EXAMPLES

Puttenham (188)
> (Water from ice,)
> It is my mother well I wot,
> And yet the daughter that I begot.

Peacham (27f)
I consume my mother that bare me I eat up my nurse that fed me, then
I die leaving them blind that saw me. . . . (a candle)
> Anatomy of wonder great I speak, and yet am dead.

Men suck sweet juice, from these black veins, which Mother wisdom bred (a book).

The vision of *Nabuchodnozor* was enigmatical, and most aptly proportioned in the similitudes, for under the form of a goodly tree, both himself and all the parts of his prosperity are most excellently described.

Cicero
Erasmus, Melancthon, Sherry, Day

Eteroeosis

Quintilian (IX, iii, 12)
Scheme. Alteration of the normal idiom.

Erasmus (38)
For plenitude of words. The use of a proper name as an adjective, or of a proper name as a pronoun.

EXAMPLE

Erasmus (38)
The Faustine letter (from *Your letter, Faustus*).

Hysterologia

Susenbrotus (32)
Scheme. It is when the preposition does not serve its related noun but appears to be subordinate to a verb, as if it were joined with the verb in one word.

Peacham (1577, Fiv)
Vice of style. When a preposition doth not serve to his casual word but is joined to a verb, as though it were compounded with it.

Puttenham (255)
Vice of style sometimes. The misplacing of words, . . . pardonable but not if the word misplaced carry any notable sense.

Peacham (Fiv)
I ran after with as much speed as I could, the thief that had undone me.
He ran against with fury rage, the doors.
When you were upon, I am sure, the top of the hill.

Puttenham (255)
A coral lip of hue.

Litotes

Susenbrotus (41)
Scheme. When we say less and mean more.

Puttenham (184)
We temper our sense with words of such moderation as in appearance
it abateth it, but not in deed.

Peacham (150)
Scheme. When the speaker by a negation equipollent doth seem to
extenuate the which he expresseth.

EXAMPLES

Puttenham (184)
He is no fool.

Peacham (150)
He is not the wisest man in the world.
It is no small account that he maketh of his own wit.
I was not the last in the field to fight against the enemies of my country.

Sherry, Day

Medela

Peacham (176)
Scheme. When seeing the offences of our friends, or of them whom we
defend, to be so great that we cannot honestly defend them, or so

manifest that we cannot well deny them, we seek to heal them with plasters of good words and pleasing speech.

EXAMPLES

Peacham (176)
When there was a greater luxury and riot objected against Caelius than Cicero durst defend . . . he did extenuate the fault with gentle words. Paul . . . in his Epistle to Philemon useth sundry reasons and diverse means to salve and cure the fault of Onesimus.

Metabole

Scaliger (IV, xxxvi)
Scheme. When we have used one word in one place, we use a different word in the corresponding place in another clause.

EXAMPLE

Scaliger (IV, xxxvi)
Quis furor ô cives? quae tanta insania? qualis est animus? quantae scelerata ad praelia vires?

Metaplasmos

Susenbrotus (19ff)
The alteration of a letter or a syllable of a word, for necessity or ornament. Forms: *prothesis* (*appositio*)—adding at the beginning; *aphoresis* (*ablatio*)—taking from the beginning; *epenthesis* (*interpositio*)—adding in the middle; *syncope* (*concisio*)—taking in the middle; *paragoge* —adding at the end; *apocope* (*absissio*)—taking at the end; *systole* (*contractio*)—a long syllable made short; *diastole*—a short syllable made long; *synalaepha* (*deletio*)—the first of two vowels off; *ethclipsis*—suppressing the consonant M and the vowel going before it; *synaeresis*—two syllables made to sound as one; *diaeresis*—when we make two two syllables of one; *antistoecon*—changing of letters; *metathesis*—when letters or syllables are transposed.

Sherry (Bvi^f)
Scheme: Adds to the list above *extensio* (*ectasis* or *tasis*), the making long of a syllable which by nature is short.

EXAMPLES

Peacham (Eiiff)
Prothesis: beknown (for *known*).
Aphoresis: headed (for *beheaded*).
Epenthesis: steadyfast (for *steadfast*).
Syncope: Hercles (for *Hercules*).
Paragoge: hasten (for *haste*).
Apocope: suspect (for *suspected*).
Systole: Diâna (for *Dïana*).
Diastole: Orphëus (for *Orphêus*).
Synalaepha: Th'offspring (for *The offspring*).
Ethclipsis: not used in English.
Synaeresis: vertuous pronounced *vertues*.
Diaeresis: Aethiopia (for *AEthiopia*).
Antistoecon: warke (for *worke*).
Metathesis: brids (for *birds*).

Quintilian
Melancthon

Paeanismos

Robortellus (49^v)
The figure of exultation used wherever poetry and oratory contain all the sorts of outbursts that express joy.

Peacham (81)
Scheme. A form of speech which the speaker useth to express his joy, either for the cause of some good thing obtained, or some evil avoided.

EXAMPLES

Peacham (81)
I will sing unto the Lord for he hath triumphed gloriously, the horse
and him that rode upon him hath he overthrown in the sea.
Henceforth all generations shall call thee blessed.

Parabola

Erasmus (73)
For plenitude of thought. A form of *exemplum*. It is a *parabola* when a
suitable similitude shows that an example [derived from things done
by nature or chance, or in some way related to man] is either similar or
dissimilar to the case in hand.

Scaliger (III, liii)
Under *tractatio*. Allegory may be considered a kind of comparison, and
that aspect of allegory which compares (the allegoric comparison) we
shall call *parabola* after the Greeks. *Parabola* includes myths and vivid
descriptions of historical events.

Peacham (1577, Mii)
Scheme. A similitude taken of those things which are done, or of those
which are joined to things by nature or hap.

Puttenham (245)
Scheme. Whenever . . . ye will seem to teach any morality or good
lesson by speeches mystical and dark or far fetched, under a sense metaphorical applying one natural thing to another, . . . inferring by them a
like consequence in other cases, . . . a resemblance mystical.

EXAMPLES

Peacham (Mii)
A ship hoisting by, taking down or winding his sails on this side, or
that side is a parable teaching a wise man to give place to times and to
accommodate and bend himself to things present.
From the Gospels, The sower went out to sow his seed etc.

Puttenham (245)
When we liken a young child to a green twig which ye may easily bend every way ye list.
All the preachings of Christ in the Gospel, as those of the wise and foolish virgins.

Quintilian, Rufinianus
Melancthon, Sherry

Paradiegesis

Quintilian (IX, ii, 107)
Scheme. Incidental narrative.

Peacham (94f)
Scheme. The orator telleth or maketh mention of something, that it may be a fit occasion or introduction to declare his further meaning, or principal purpose, which is a special and artificial form of insinuation. . . . The narration must be like to the purpose that shall follow.

EXAMPLE

Peacham (94)
Ye men of Athens, I perceive that in all things ye are too superstitious, for as I passed by, I found an altar wherein is written unto the unknown GOD whom ye then ignorantly worship, him show I unto you, God that made the world, and all things that are therein, seeing he is Lord of heaven and earth, dwelleth not in temples made by hands, neither is worshipped with men's hands.

Parelcon

Susenbrotus (30)
Scheme. When for the sake of ornament a word is extended at the end by the addition of a syllable.

Peacham (1577, Fiii)
Scheme. When a syllable is added to the end of a word, or when two words are joined together in one.

EXAMPLES

Peacham (Fiii)
Forwhy I could not otherwise do (not *for*).
Whenthat I call (not *when*).

Parodia

Quintilian (IX, ii, 34f)
Scheme. We may introduce imaginary writings . . . The name *parodia* is drawn from songs sung in imitation of others but employed to designate imitation in verse or prose.

EXAMPLE

Quintilian (IX, ii, 34f)
Let my mother who was the object of my love and my delight, . . . inherit nought of my property: (imitating an document produced by the opposing party 'Let Publius Novanus Gallo, to whom as my bene-factor I will and owe all that is good . . . be my heir'.

Periergia

Quintilian (VIII, iii, 55)
Vice. Superfluous elaboration which differs from its corresponding virtue much as fussiness differs from industry, and superstition from religion.

Peacham (1577, Giii^v)
Vice. When in a small matter, there is too much labour bestowed, and too many words and figures used, which they do use most commonly, that do fondly covet copy, and take greater care to paint their speech with fine words, than to express the truth plainly.

Puttenham (258)
Vice. Superfluity of travail to describe the matter which ye take in hand . . . the curious.

EXAMPLE

Puttenham (258)
>   The tenth of March when Aries received
>   Dan Phoebus rays into his horned head,
>   And I myself by learned lore perceived
>   That Ver approached and frosty winter fled
>   I crost the Thames to take the cheerful air,
>   In open fields, the weather was so fair.

Veltkirchius, Sherry

Peristasis

Erasmus (57)
For plenitude of thought. When we enlarge by expounding the circumstances of our subject, its cause, occasion, instrument, time, mode, etc. . . . Advantageous in amplifying, . . . in vivid representation, . . . in confirming an argument.

Peacham (164)
Scheme. A form of speech by which the orator amplifieth by circumstances, either of a person or a thing.

EXAMPLES

Peacham (165)
Boldness, unchaste speech, manlike apparel and gesture are all unseemly in woman, and womankind. (Person, from the circumstance of sex.)

Peacham (166)
They bought and sold in the temple the house of prayer, and therefore they were reputed thieves, and the temple called their den. (Thing, from the circumstance of place.)

Quintilian

Prosodiasaphesis

Scaliger (IV, xxxiv)
Scheme. When something small is added by way of explication, as are
many epithets which appear superfluous. . . . The purpose of this is to
add a reason or . . . an exposition of the situation.

EXAMPLE
Scaliger (IV, xxxiv)
They say that he for a whole seven months on end mopes in solitude.

Scesisonomaton

Susenbrotus (38)
Scheme. When each single noun is accompanied by a single adjective.

Peacham (1577, Giv^v)
Scheme. When a sentence or saying do consist altogether of nouns, as
when to every substantive an adjective is joined.

EXAMPLE
Peacham (Giv^v)
A man faithful in friendship, prudent in counsels, virtuous in conversation, gentle in communication, learned in all liberal sciences,
eloquent in utterance, comely in gesture, pitiful to the poor, an enemy
to naughtiness, a lover of all virtue and godliness.

Solecismos

Ad Herennium (IV, 17)
When the concord between a word and the one before it in a group of
words is faulty.

Puttenham (251)
Vice. When we speak false English; that is by misusing the grammatical rules to be observed in cases, genders, tenses etc.

Quintilian
Veltkirchius, Sherry

Synchoresis

Peacham (III)
Scheme. The orator, trusting strongly to his cause, giveth leave to the judges or to his adversaries to consider of it with indifference, and so to judge of it, if it be found just and good, to allow it, if evil, to condemn and punish it.

EXAMPLES

Peacham (III)
But now Judges I leave the whole, and the most lawful right of my cause, which I have declared, and commit it unto you to judge and determine it, as reason and wisdom shall direct you.
Whether it be right in the sight of God to hearken unto you more than unto God, judge ye.

Topothesia

Erasmus (54)
The description of a fictional place so as to bring it before the eye.
Susenbrotus (88)
Scheme. The depiction of an imaginary, non-existant place not to be found among known lands.

Peacham (141f)
Scheme. A feigned description of a place, that is when the orator describeth a place, and yet no such place. . . . This figure is proper to poets and is seldom used of orators.

EXAMPLES

Peacham (141)
The house of Envy in the sixth book of *Metamorphoses.*
The house of sleep in the eleventh book.

Sherry, Puttenham

Style

THE THREE DIVISIONS OF STYLE

Adros (Supra, Magniloquens)

The great or mighty kind, when we use great words, or vehement figures (Wilson 169).
Always dignified and sonorous. . . . Figures which are used especially in the grand style are *circumlocutio, transmutatio,* and *metabole* (Scaliger IV, xvi).

Ichnos (Infinum, Humile)

The low kind when we use no metaphors nor translated words, nor yet use any amplifications, but go plainly to work, and speak altogether in common words (Wilson 169).

Mesos (Aequabile, Mediocre)

The small kind, when we moderate our heat by meaner words, and use not the most stirring sentences (Wilson 169).

This style is flexible, subtle and succint. It may at times be bare. It uses figures but it does not use many. Its proper qualities are fullness and ease (Scaliger IV, xxi).

ASPECTS OF STYLE

Acre

Something is sharp which is pointed. It not only disturbs but also nags, ... and indeed in the Aeneid all expressions of sarcasm are sharp (Scaliger IV, xv).

Acutus

The quality of style by which what is said is evidently witty and full of bite (Scaliger, IV, xiv).

Adianomta

Expressions which have a secret meaning. . . . Such expressions are regarded as . . . eloquent simply because of their ambiguity and quite a number of persons have become infected by the belief that a passage which requires a commentator must for that very reason be a master-piece of elegance (Quintilian VIII, ii, 20f).

Affectus

The Renaissance term for 'stylistic quality', or 'characteristic of style'. Some qualities such as clarity must be present in all styles; others are peculiar to the grand, the medium or the low style: others are required only upon occasion. *Acre* and *acutus* are *affectus*.

Ambitio (Cacozelia)

Perverse affectation is a fault in every kind of style: it includes all that is turgid, trivial, luscious, redundant, far-fetched or extravagant. The same name is also applied to virtues carried to excess when the mind loses its critical sense and is misled by the false appearance of beauty (Quintilian VIII, iii, 56f).

Aspera

The opposite of the gentle or harmonious, offensive to the ear (Scaliger IV, i).

Brevitas

Terse expression using short sentences, the brevity that says nothing more than is absolutely necessary. It may be employed with admirable results when it expresses a great deal in a very few words (Quintilian, VIII, iii, 82).

Celeriter

To give a much stronger imitation of the real, we use the speed that . . . corresponds to that demanded by the meaning (Scaliger, IV, xlvi).

Claritas

A style composed with purity and ease, in which each of the elements present leads to clarity. . . . The arguments are general, understood by everybody and self-evident. . . . The words similarly are in general use and are used in their proper senses, not metaphorically. . . . Nevertheless they are drawn from educated rather than colloquial discourse (Trissino Bi^v-Bii).

Coloratum (Pingue, Pichiologia)

Objectionable overexuberance. . . . This kind of writing displays the desire of the writer to do more than he can and his failure to achieve what minimally he must; in short, the style that pretends to more than it performs. (Scaliger, IV, xxiv).

P
215

Copia

Plenitude of thoughts and words, the opposite of brevity. The copious style speaks most fully, and enriches its matter with as varied an ornamentation as possible, expanding the subject until nothing can be added to it (Erasmus 11ff).

Cultus

The purging of anything gross or mean from the elegant style. The result is that we refrain from saying everything that we could say, and from using every word that we could use. Hence this style is called terse (Scaliger IV, iv).

Dignitas

When no feature of the grand style deviates from the grandiloquent. This is not only a matter of speaking but also a quality of men. . . . It consists in gravity of subject matter and sublimity of diction (Scaliger IV, xvi).

Energia

Vigour, . . . its peculiar function in securing that nothing that we say is tame (Quintilian VIII, iii, 89).

Evidentia (Enargia)

Vivid illustration or representation is something more than mere clearness, since the latter merely lets itself be seen whereas the former thrusts itself upon our notice. . . . The facts . . . are displayed in their living truth to the eyes of the mind (Quintilian VIII, iii, 61f).
This style does not state a thing simply but sets it forth to be viewed as though portrayed in colour . . . so that it may seem to be painted, not narrated (Erasmus 47).

Floridum

A form of plenitude which adds matter and ornament that could be withdrawn without loss to the meaning. The addition is for decoration, . . . which can produce incomparable ornamentation (Scaliger IV, ix).

Foedus

Servius says that this quality of style is not obscenity so much as crudity. I maintain however that it is also obscenity (Scaliger IV, xvi).

Gravitas

A quality of the grand style, . . . of both matter and diction, where the arrangement of word with word itself has dignity. Dignified words are those which do not sink to the level of ordinary usage (Scaliger IV, xviii).

Humilia

A fault. Language may be described as mean when it is beneath the dignity of the subject or the rank of the speaker (Quintilian VIII, ii, 2).

Incitatio

When ideas and expressions are linked one after another. This is not a rhetorical figure but it is conducive to the use of a figure, *asyndeton* (Scaliger IV, xii).

Languida (Paresin)

A fault, a style lacking vigour. It slips from the ear and leaves no mark at all. It is entirely without bite and wit (Scaliger III, xxvii).

Licentia

A vicious form of writing, when the writer utilises any and every form regardless of the power it might have only in a certain place. From this we get rattling words and rough discordant patches (Scaliger IV, xxiv).

Magna

A quality of diction—dignity or height of style. It is achieved by a style in which great matters are presented with incisiveness, vehemence, splendour and vigour, . . . and which avoids any common usage or mean construction. . . . It does not use special words but depends on the manner of using ordinary words, rhetorical figures and metrical patterns (Trissino Bii^v-Biii^v).

Molle

A quality of diction. An arrangement of words that does not offend the ear but yields to our sense of harmony, thus easily gaining admittance to the mind and retaining its hold upon the memory (Scaliger IV, x).

Negligentia

A vice of the low style. Negligence gives the worst qualities to an oration, and allows it not merely to crawl but even to collapse (Scaliger IV, xxiv).

Numerositas

It is, as nature and reason tell us, the soul of poetry. . . . It makes the low style more simple, the medium more persuasive, the grand more effective (Scaliger IV, vii).

Obscuritas

Obscurity results from the employment of obsolete words and the use of dialect words. A greater source of obscurity is found in the construction and combination of words, in sentences which are too long, in excessive *hyperbaton*, *interjectio*, in ambiguity. A fault (Quintilian VIII, ii, 12ff).

A quality of diction, the opposite of perspicuity (Scaliger IV, i).

Perspicuitas

Clearness or perspicuity results above all from the use of the proper and exact words. . . . Clearness is the first essential of a good style: there must be propriety in our words, their order must be straightforward, the conclusion of the period must not be long postponed, there must be nothing lacking and nothing superfluous (Quintilian VIII, ii).

Plenitudo

The quality of a style in which nothing which could possibly be wanted is lacking, everything is freely enlarged upon and yet nothing is redundant (Scaliger IV, viii).

Proprietas

A quality of diction and style. Propriety means calling things by their right names. . . . Propriety turns not on the actual term but on the meaning of the term and must be tested by the understanding not the ear. . . . There is a form of propriety of speech which deserves the highest praise: the employment of words with the maximum of significance (Quintilian VIII, ii, lff).

Pulchritudo

A quality of diction. A kind of perfection in which the whole is beautiful because the parts are symmetrical. . . . In the part it consists in delectable and harmonious colours and figures; in the whole in the harmony of the parts by mode, figure, place, number and colour. . . . Everything depends on proportion: from proportion we get harmony, and from harmony, beauty (Scaliger IV, i).

Pura

A quality of diction, in which no word is foreign and no word is low or mean (Scaliger IV, i).

Puritas

A quality of style, often but not always a quality of the low style. It is in part a bareness, admitting no ornament. . . . It differs from simplicity which describes things simply, without antecedant or circumstance. *Puritas* is a style without ornament (Scaliger IV, xiii).

Rotunditas

A quality of the medium style. Nothing in this style is even or feeble: neither is anything turgid or angular (Scaliger IV, xxii).

Securitas

A quality sometimes found in the low style: the consistent adherence to a common and direct mode of presentation (Scaliger IV, xx).

Sicca (Aschematismus)

A fault, when the oration is all plain and simple, and lacketh his figures, whereby as it were with stars it might shine (Sherry Cii).

Simplicitas

A pure style without tropes. It is appropriate to the low style (although not continuously but when time and place demand) (Scaliger IV, xx).

Sonus

A quality of the grand style. It is a unique voice (*the* voice of the grand style) and not a kind of voice, nor merely the sound resulting from the use of feet and metre (Scaliger IV, xvii).

Splendor

A quality of style; the opposite of *puritas*. . . . It is at its most intense when it strikes out like a light from any discourse of praise as the sun strikes the faculty of vision. . . . With *splendor* we have a certain freedom of diction, which can be drawn from any source (Scaliger IV, i).

Suavitas

A quality of style. When a charming appearance is commended by being in every part delicate. Sweet speech is that which entices the reader to read even against his will. . . . In fact sweetness is a delicate form of *venustas* (charm) (Scaliger IV, xi).

Tediosum (Nulla varietas, Homologia)

A fault: when the whole matter is all alike, and hath no variety to avoid tediousness (Sherry Ci).

Tenuitas

A quality of the low style. The bare speech consists only of words, syntactic forms and expressions drawn from ordinary and common speech (Scaliger IV, xx).

Trepidatio

The corrupted form of the medium style since when this style is subdued it becomes thin and when it dares to rise it becomes swollen (Scaliger IV, xxiv).

Tumiditas (Bomboliogia)

A fault: the Asiatic speech, full of immoderately used words and figures to set forth matter which is stupid and inane, using, for example, splendid words to write to a farmer (Veltkirchius 10).

Urbanitas

Urbanitas involves the total absence of all that is incongruous, coarse, unpolished and exotic whether in thought, language, voice or gesture and resides not so much in isolated sayings as in the whole complexion of our language (Quintilian VI, iii, 107).

Vacui

A quality of sound, when either through observing a principle of composition or from the nature of the word itself a word appears to draw apart from the other words, leaving a pause not between the metrical units but between the words. The use of this at frequent intervals increases the emotional effect of a statement (Scaliger IV, xlvi).

Vehementia

A quality sometimes found in the grand style. True forcefulness comes not so much from the content of a work as from the words, the phrases, the metre and the rhetorical figures used. It comes particularly from an arrangement of words which slightly impedes the pronunciation, . . . often at the beginning or the end of a particular section (Scaliger IV, xviii).

Velocitas

A quality of diction. An arrangement of words with which the work moves rapidly forward, such as is found in lively and flexible speech (Scaliger IV, i).

Venustas

A quality of style, charm. In the low style, this quality is manifested in firmness and compact brevity; in the medium style as copiousness and elaborateness; in the grand style as high artifice. . . . It is also described as *prudentia*, sureness of judgement in the selection of words and figures (Scaliger IV, vi).

Veritas

A quality of diction. When we select words which are simple and seem to express what we actually feel, thus making the work of fiction seem more immediate and almost real (Trissino Cii).

Volubilitas

A quality of the medium style, one which flows thinly when used with the low style, but with an exalted and elevated style, it remains and lingers in the ears and in the mind (Scaliger IV, xxii).

Genre

Allegoria

This is a species of narrative. It is not a simple narrative but one which invites a second, different interpretation, alluding to things from quite another sequence of events and to moral attitudes, emotions or types of character present. One kind of allegory is called mythology, the interpretation and explanation of myths. . . . Allegory is also the method of exposition of prophecies, divinations, prodigies, signs and dreams (Veltkirchius 146f).

Apologia

The generic term for any extended narrative structure. There are eight kinds: fable, myth, drama, history, rhetorical narrative, moral narrative, allegory and exegetic commentary (Veltkirchius 145ff).

Aprobaterion

A poem or speech for the departure of some person which usually includes a praise of this person's nation or country and their reason for leaving (Scaliger III, cvii).

Canzone

A verbal composition with a harmony regulated by certain numbers and metres woven and ordered and made appropriate to the song, . . . a form of composition magnificent and splendid (Minturno 186).

Carmen correlativum

A symmetrical form of composition, whereby one can have a series of corresponding words in each verse, or a recapitulation of several terms previously stated singly, etc. (Scaliger II, xxx).

Comedia

A variety of drama which does not present kings and heroes but instead games, revels, weddings, the tricks of slaves, drunkenness, and deceptions practised upon older men. . . . The ending may be *unhappy* for some of the characters concerned. The comedies we most prize are those which cause us to condemn the vices represented. . . . Often they open with a separate prologue and close with a chorus (Scaliger III, xcvii).

Drama

One of the species of *apologia*. In drama the exposition is entirely by direct speech, as in comedies, tragedies, bucolics, eclogues (Veltkirchius 145^v).

Elegia

The material of this genre may be either lugubrious, as in the commiserations of lovers . . . or celebratory as in songs of thanks, or of successful amatory conquest. . . . The nature of the elegy is candid, terse, and perspicuous and it is neither affected nor precious. It is characterised by its own rather free form of pentameter (Scaliger, III, cxxv and IV, xlix).

Epibaterion

A song sung on the arrival of an illustrious person after a voyage. Its beginning is a praise of the prince of his particular country. . . . The places of invention used include the aspects of this region, its rivers, buildings, cities and so on. . . . It is in the grand style (Scaliger III, cvi).

Epigrammatum

A brief poem or inscription which plainly describes some person, thing or fact and which is useful for definition or dilemma. . . . It may be obscene, trivial or amusing, noble or generous. . . . It belongs to either the low or the medium style (Scaliger VI, cxxvi).

Epitaph

A poem for a dead person, on the occasion of their death or of the anniversary of it. . . . Its parts include a praise of the subject, a demonstration of the effect of his loss, consolation to his mourners and an exhortation to remember him and to profit by his example (Scaliger III, cxxii).

Epithalamion

The wedding poem. It celebrates the place, the event, the persons and their good fortune. . . . It has three parts; the *desponsalia* celebrating the betrothal, the *debucatia* celebrating the marriage and *repotia*, celebrating the wedding feast. . . . The question of defloration may be avoided by calling the bride a matron; . . . alternatively attention may be directed toward the feast, Hymen and his chorus speak and in this way defloration is brought in (Scaliger III, ci).

Ethopoeia

An exposition of moral precepts: a moral argument. The *ethopoeia* should be slow, grave and should contain similes describing emotional states (Veltkirchius 146).

Exergasia

A species of *apologia*. An added narration which introduces other matter or expounds some aspect of the original rext. The latter we call commentaries, such as those of Servius and Donatus on Virgil. . . . There are three modes of *exergasia*; a brief summary or exposition, . . . paraphrases (or synonymous expressions to present the meaning) . . . and the presentation of the meaning through additional matter, both paraphrasing and giving a more plentiful commentary (Veltkirchius 146^{v}f).

Fabella

A species of *apologia*, in which we attribute speech, emotion, and human customs to inanimate things, and mute animals as in the fables of Aesop (Veltkirchius 145^v) [see also the figure FABELLA].

Fabula (Mythos)

A species of apologia. A poetic narrative which describes not things which are real but things which are at a great distance from the real, . . . as in, for example, the *Metamorphoses* of Ovid (Veltkirchius 145^v) [see also the figure FABULA].

Genethliaca

Poems about the birth of great men. . . . One can start with oracles, auguries or the dreams of parents. . . . Common topics include the day, the time, the season (Scaliger III, cii).

Heroica (Epic)

This is the one, perfect kind of poem, the original for all the other kinds. . . . It contains within it the universal and controlling rules for the composition of *each* kind, according at each point to the nature of the ideas present and the style appropriate to each subject. . . . Its parts grow organically together, paralleling the structures of nature. . . . Its themes are from the life of man and concern important persons, kings and heroes. However gods may come into the poem, to negotiate or act (Scaliger III, xcvi).

Historia

A species of *apologia* which relates that which is true, and pleasurable or instructive to know. Its themes include virtues, vices, counsels, events and the sayings of great men, . . . as in the works of Livy, Sallust and Herodotus (Veltkirchius 145ᵛ).

Hymnos

Mystic songs in praise of God, or other supernatural powers known as gods. . . . The species of hymn include: *kletikoi*, invoking a god; . . . *apopemplikoi*, valedictions to a god; . . . *psysikoi*, calling upon the presiding deity of day, night, tempest or justice, law, virtue, honour, fame etc. (Scaliger III, cxiiff).

Laus

A poem or piece in praise of a person, place, time or thing. Its species include *epanos* in praise of virtue, . . . *aeolica* which deals with simple things, praising the simple and true in a brief style without ornament, . . . *macarismos* in praise of blessed men, . . . *adamonismos* praising the gods (Scaliger III, cx).

Lyrica

Whatever can be represented in a short poem lyrics have described; praises, loves, disputes, things not done, feasts, wishes, vows. . . . They may narrate brief events, desires, conquests or explain places and times or repudiate suspicions, or present invitations and expressions of disgust. Frequently they are about love. . . . Their delightfulness (according to Horace) lies in their brevity (Scaliger III, cxxiv).

Mime

A dramatic form descended from the Old Comedy. . . . It uses parody and in it any kind of thing may speak; a person, an animal or a god. . . . It has no choruses and no acts. The characters are from the lower classes (fullers, butchers, bootmakers etc.). Its subjects are fraud, crime, the jests of rustics, things plebian. It features pandering, jokes, disguise (Scaliger III, xcvii).

Narratio rhetorica

A species of apologia. A brief exposition of fact, used particularly in legal or scholastic oratory, in which we explain, make as clear as possible, and fully describe the nature of our material (Veltkirchius 146).

Oaristys

A poem which celebrates married bliss. . . . The material it contains, the arguments, the precepts it puts forward are all various, depending upon the nature of the persons concerned, whether they are citizens, soldiers or rustics (Scaliger III, cii).

Padeuteria

A poem giving thanks to teachers for what we have been taught, or to God for our teachers. . . . In it we may use illustrious comparisons such as, for example, Socrates or Aristotle (Scaliger III, cviii).

Panegyricon

Poems of celebration and praise. . . . These are in the grand style, and are not to be used for common topics. They must not be too erudite, and must be without ostentation or arrogance. . . . One mode is comparative, . . . the comparisons often being drawn from myth. . . . The panegyric is a speech of praise to be given before a large audience (Scaliger III, cix).

Pastoralia

The subjects of the pastoral include ploughing, harvest, mowing, the cutting of wood, wayfaring, the lives of sheep and goatherds, vegetable growers, fishing and country houses. They contain arguments, rejoicings, amorous entreaty, love songs, monodies, vows, recitals of deeds, rustic celebrations, praises, *oaristiae*, wooings or disputes in praise of different girls. . . . What the poet wishes to disguise he may convey by means of rustic personae. Sylvan poems therefore are not a despised form of art. *Idylls* are short, unpretentious poems (Scaliger, I, iv and III, xcix).

Propempticon

Poems of honour to the departed (including funerals); to their country, office, friends, etc. They treat of the time and place of farewell, of the office left, . . . of the voyage, . . . of the place to which the one departing goes, of his colleagues, his fellows, and his men (Scaliger III, civ).

Recantatio (Palinodia)

This was in antiquity the genealogy of a hero or a list of his deeds. It was believed to be true. . . . The palinode resembles the hymn, except that its subject is a hero, not a god (Scaliger III, cxvi).

Satyra

This is one genre whose species are divided by the manner of presentation; simple narrative (as in Juvenal), dramatic monologue without the persona of the poet, or a mixed narrative. Satires are also differentiated in character—Juvenal burns, Horace laughs, Persius insults—or by their nature—grave, ridiculous or varied. . . . They have no set parts, and begin abruptly with no *proemion*. The satirist is allowed great licence. . . . His diction is common, colloquial, obscene and familiar. . . . The range of style is from the low to the medium according to the subject treated (Scaliger III, xcviii).

Sonnet

A serious but delicate composition with rhymes and syllables contained in a certain number of verses and under certain limiting rules. . . . Without lightness and beauty the sonnet is worthless. . . . Its argument must be restricted to a few lines. . . . Its diction should be carefully selected, and beautifully and elegantly arranged. The sentiments expressed are serious or intense or sweet. . . . Its purpose may be to narrate, pray, comfort, express scorn, praise or blame (Minturno 240f).

Sylva

This kind of poem deals with many different matters, often with the inculcating of learning or with first principles. It may be primitive, effusive or harshly critical (Scaliger III, c).

Tragedia

This form of drama rarely includes persons of low degree. . . . Its argument is taken from historical material from which it does not greatly vary. . . . The two pillars supporting tragedy are the simple and precise statement, . . . the figured or dramatic form of exposition. . . . Its purpose is to teach and move and delight, as well as to please by its spectacle. . . . Its argument should be brief and complex. The dead may be introduced as ghosts. . . . It may have more than one important event (that is, plural action) (Scaliger III, xcvii).

Vituperatio

A speech which exposes the bad. . . . We can castigate those things we can praise—people, things, times, places, animals, plants and so on. We can castigate things singly or in groups. [The parts of a vituperative speech include a *proemion*, a division into kinds, a treatment of different aspects of our subject such as deeds or education, an epilogue] (Aphthonius Bvi^vf).

Bibliography

A CHECKLIST OF RHETORICAL TEXTBOOKS IN USE IN
SIXTEENTH-CENTURY SCHOOLS AND UNIVERSITIES [1]

AEMSTELREDAMUS, ALARDUS,   *Selectae aliquot similitudines, sive collationes tum
ex Biblis sacris, tum ex veterum orthodoxum commentariis* (Cologne 1539).

AGRICOLA, RODOLPHUS, *Aphthonius sophistae progymnasmata Rodolpho Agricola
Phrisio interprete* (Bonn 1507).[2]

ANGELI, R. C., *Tabulae rhetoricae, quibus omnia quae ab Aristotele tribus, de arte
dicendis libris, et a Demetrio Phalero suo de elocutione libello tradita sunt*
(Venice 1571).

BALBUS, JOANNES, *Catholicon* (Venice 1506).

BEUMLERIUS, MARIUS, *Elocutiones rhetoricae libri duo* (Zurich 1598).

BLEBEL, THOMAS, *Rhetorica artis progymnasmata . . . ad puerilem institutionem
accomodatur* (Leipzig 1584).

BUCOLDIANUS, GERALDUS, *De inventione et amplificatione oratoria, seu usu locorum
libri tres* (Lyons 1551).

---

[1] The editions cited here are early, although not necessarily the first.

[2] Classical texts published in the Renaissance I have listed under the names of
typical editors and commentators or, when they appeared in collections, under the
name of the author.

233

BUTLER, CHARLES, *Rhetoricae libri duo* (Oxford 1598).

CAESARIUS, JOANNES, *Rhetorica in septum libros* (Paris 1538).

CAMERARIUS, JOACHIM, *Aphthonius Sophista libellus progymnasmatum in sermonem Latinum conversus, Graeco scripto et exemplis compluribus additio a Joach. Camerario* (Leipzig 1567).

Elementa rhetoricae (Basle 1540).

Notatio figurarum orationis et mutatae simplicis elocutionis in Apostolicis scriptis (Leipzig 1556).

Primae apud rhetorem exercitationes Theon sophistae Joachim Camerarii in sermonem Latinum conversae (Basle 1541).

CASSANDER, GEORGIUS, *Tabulae breves in praeceptiones rhetoricas* (Antwerp 1548).

CASSIODORUS, MARCUS AURELIUS, 'Rhetoricae compendium', in *Antiqui rhetores* (Paris 1599).

CELTUS, CONRAD, *Index rhetorices ex Cicerone* (Strasbourg 1578).

CURIO, CAELIUS SECUNDUS, *Ciceronis trium de Oratore librorum summa absolutissima* (Frankfurt 1567).

CYLLENIUS, RAPH, *Tabulae rhetoricae* (Venice 1571).

DESPAUTERIUS, JOANNES, *De figuris liber ex Quintilliano, Donato, Diomede, Valla, Placentino, etc.* (Lyons 1526).

DOELSCH, JOHN, *In D. Erasmus libros de duplici copia verborum ac rerum commentariis M. Veltkirchii* (Paris 1539).

DU FLOS, J. *Rhetoricarum praeceptionum tabulae* (Paris 1554).

ERASMUS, DESIDERIUS, *De duplici copia verborum ac rerum commentari duo* (Basle 1521).

Opus de conscribendus epistolis (Basle 1522).

ERYTHRAEUS, VALENTINUS, *Commentarii notationis artificii rhetorici ac dialectici in orationem Ciceronis pro A. Licinio Archia* (Strasbourg 1550).

De Grammaticorum figuris libri quatuor; liber unus de vitiis orationis (Strasbourg 1561).

De elocutione libri tres, confecti ex quarto ad Herennium, Cicerone et Hermogene (Strasbourg 1567).

Microtekin, seu medulla rhetoricae Tullianae, e corpore librorum Ciceronis de doctrina dicendi; libri tres (Norimberg 1575).

FLORENTINUS, LAURENTIUS, *In libro de elocutione* (Venice 1561).

FREIGIUS, J. T., *Trium artium logicarum, grammaticae, dialecticae et rhetoricae, breve succinctique schematismi* (Basle 1568).

Rhetorica, poetica, logica ad usum rudicorum in epitomem redacta (Norimberg 1594).

GUNTHERUS, PETRUS, *De arte rhetorica libri duo* (Strasbourg 1568).

HAZARDIÈRE, P. DE LA, *Summa rhetoricae* (Paris c. 1475).

KIRCHNER, L., *Medulla praeceptionum rhetoricarum* (Coburg 1594).

LATOMUS, BARTHOLOMAEUS, *Summa totius rationis dissevendi et dialecticas et rhetoricas partes complectens* (Cologne 1527).

LILY, WILLIAM, *De octu orationis partium constructione* (Strasbourg 1515).

LONGOLIUS, GILBERTUS, *Rhetoricorum ad C. Herennium libri tres, de inventione rhetorica libri duo cum M. Fabii Victorini commentariis*, with annotations by Longolius (Cologne 1539).

LORICHIUS, REINHARDUS, *Aphthonii Sophistae progymnasmata . . . cum luculentis et utilibus in eadem scholiis Reinhardi Lorichii Hadamari* (London 1572).

MACROPEDIUS, GEORGIUS, *Methodus de conscribendis epistolis* (London 1580).

MAIOR, GEORGIUS, *In Philipi Melancthoniis rhetorica tabulae, una cum tabula de schematibus et tropis Petri Mosellani* (Strasbourg 1529).

MELANCTHON, PHILIP, *De rhetorica libri tres* (Wittenburg 1519).

Elementorum rhetorices libri duo (Paris 1532).

Institutiones rhetoricae (The Hague 1521).

M. Tulli Ciceronis de oratore libri tres, a Philippo Melancthone scholiis ac notulis quibusdam illustrati (Paris 1539).

MOSELLANUS, PETRUS (see under SCHADE).

NIPHUS, AUGUSTINUS, *Epitomata rhetorica ludicra* (Venice 1521).

OMPHIALUS, JACOBUS, *De elocutionis imitatione ac apparatu liber* (Paris 1579).

PEREZ, JUAN, *Progymnasmata artis rhetoricae* (Alcala 1539).

PRISCIANUS GRAMMATICUS, *De praeexercitamentis rhetoricae ex Hermogene translatis* (c. 1475).

PUBLICIUS, JACOBUS, *Oratoria artis epitomata* (Venice 1485).

REUSNER, NICOLAS, *Elementorum artis rhetoricae* (Strasbourg 1578).

RICCOBONI, ANTONIO, *Paraphrasis in rhetoricam Aristotele* (Frankfurt 1588).

Commentarius quo . . . explicatur doctrina librorum de inventione, partitionem, topicorum, oratoris ad Brutum, librorum de oratore (Venice 1567).

RINGELBERG, J. F., *Liber de figuris ac vitiis orationis* (Lyons 1531).

RIVIUS, JOANNES, *De rhetorica libri duo* (Louvain 1550).

Rhetorica (Paris 1537).

Rhetoricae et quae ad eam spectant (Lyons 1531).

SCHADE, PETER, *De primus apud rhetorem exercitationibus, praeceptiones in studiorum usum comparata* (Cologne 1523).

Tabulae de schematibus et tropis (Antwerp 1529).

Tabulae de schematibus et tropis in rhetorica in Erasmi Roterdami libellum de duplici copia (Strasbourg 1529).

SEVERIANUS, JULIUS, 'Syntomata sive praecepta artis rhetoricae summatim collecta de multis' in *Antiqui rhetores* (Paris 1599).

SOAREZ, CYPRIANUS, *De arte rhetorica libri tres, ex Aristotele, Cicerone, et Quinctiliano praecipue deprompti* (Verona 1589).

Tabulae rhetorica (Venice 1589).

STOCKWOOD, JOHN, *Progymnasma scholasticum* (London 1597).

STREBAEUS, J. L., *De verborum electione et collocatione oratoria* (Basle 1539).

STURMIUS, JOANNES, *Hermogenes de dicendi generibus sive formis orationem liber duo, latinate donatus et scholis explicatus atque illustratus* (Strasbourg 1570).

Hermogenes partitionem rhetoricarum liber uno . . . latinate donatus et scholis explicatus atque illustratus (Strasbourg 1570).

Scholia ad rhetorica Aristotelis (Strasbourg 1570).

Tabulae partitionem oratorium Ciceronis et quatuor dialogorum . . . et scholiae aeconomicae Erythrai (Strasbourg 1560).

SUSENBROTUS, JOANNES, *Epitome troporum ac schematum et grammaticorum et rhetorum* (Zurich 1541).

SYLVIUS, FRANCISCUS, *Progymnasmatum in artem oratoriam* (Paris 1520).

TARDIF, GUILLAUME, *Rhetoricae artis ac oratoriae facultatis compendium* (Paris c. 1475).

TORRES, ALFONSO, *Tabula in rhetoricam* (Alcala 1569).

VALERIUS, CORNELIUS, *In universam bene dicendi rationem tabula, summam artis rhetoricae complectens* (Antwerp 1568).

Rhetorica ad majorem purerorum commoditatem per interrogationes et responsiones digesta (Antwerp 1596).

VEREPAEUS, SIMON, *Praeceptiones de figuris seu de tropis et schematibus, in communem scholarum usum* (Cologne 1590).

Praeceptiones de verborum et rerum copia (Cologne 1590).

WOLFIUS, HIERONYMUS, *Progymnasma scholasticum in aliquot Ciceronis sententias* (Basle 1580).

VIVES, JUAN LUIS, *De conscribendus epistolis argumenti D. Erasmi compendium* (Wittenburg 1536).

De ratione dicendi, libri tres (Louvain 1533).

CRITICAL BIBLIOGRAPHY OF IMPORTANT RENAISSANCE TEXTS

ERASMUS, DESIDERIUS, *De duplici copia verborum ac rerum commentari duo* (Basle 1521). A text on the means of obtaining richness of style, both by a large possible choice of words and a large store of ideas. This is a simple but extremely intelligent text drawing mainly upon Quintilian but rearranged to display the material with a new, less strictly forensic emphasis.

FICHETUS, GULIEMUS, *Rhetorica* (Paris 1471). A traditional treatise following the organisation about the headings Judicial, Deliberative and Demonstrative of Trapezuntius. Fichetus was a famous teacher of the Sorbonne.

HARVEY, GABRIEL, *Ciceronianus* (London 1577). This lecture inveighs against the system of studying Cicero through the commentators and recommends the study of 'the stores of argument . . . and the structural framework' instead of the ornaments alone. Harvey argues for a pedagogic simplification to follow Ramus' pruning of logic.

Rhetor . . . de natura, arte et exercitatione rhetorica (London 1577). These two lectures recommend, instead of the standard and dull school texts of Susenbrotus and Mosellanus, the study of the rhetoric of Talaeus backed up by reading the works of Cicero, Quintilian, Ramus and Vives.

MELANCTHON, PHILIP, *De Rhetorica libri tres* (Wittenburg 1519). The bulk of this treatise is given over to *inventio* and follows Trapezuntius. The section on *elocutio* contains Quintilian's four schemes for amplification, 13 tropes and 30 other schemes. The figures are discussed very briefly.

Institutiones rhetoricae (The Hague 1521). The third section on *elocutio* presents the figures with a confused attempt at a logical classification, by the word, the sentence and amplification (pertaining to larger units). The tropes and schemes are presented as tropes and schemes of a single word or of a phrase. This classification appears (among others) in Susenbrotus, a very popular school text.

ROBORTELLUS, FRANCISCUS, *De artificio dicendi* (Bonn 1567). A collection of essays upon different aspects of *elocutio*, many of which are definitions gathered as a result of investigation into the origin and significance of obscure terms. Other chapters compare the treatment of a particular topic in different texts.

SCALIGER, JULIUS CAESAR, *Poetices libri septem* (Lyons 1561). An exhaustive work on poetry containing one book which deals with the figures of rhetoric as devices of style. Scaliger's classification of the figures is an attempt at some organic way of dealing with them, and they are grouped according to their literary effect, whether it be to describe, expand or omit. Scaliger regards almost all rhetorical devices as tropes, that is, figures whose effect depends upon some variation away from the ordinary meaning of a word. This work also contains an important section on style.

SEBASTIANI, ANTONIO (MINTURNO), *L'arte poetica* (Venice 1564). This vernacular treatise on Tuscan poetry is more important for its sections on style and its description of contempory Italian genres such as the *canzone* and the sonnet than for its treatment of rhetoric.

STURMIUS, JOANNES, *De universa ratione elocutionis rhetoricae libri tres* (Strasbourg 1576). This is an exhaustive treatise on *elocutio*, derived from almost every classical authority known to the Renaissance. Sturmius covers eight divisions of *elocutio* (*sententia, sententia conformatio, verba, verborum ornamenta, membra, verborum consecutiones, clausulae, numeras*) in tremendous detail. The subject as treated here is the extreme point of the protestant pedagogic tendency towards complexity of detail.

TALAEUS, AUDOMARUS, *Institutiones oratoriae* (Paris 1545).

Rhetorica (Paris 1548). The *Rhetorica* is a revised version of the *Institutiones*.[1] It is the original Ramistic treatise on rhetoric. Following Ramus' contention that *inventio* and *dispositio* belong properly to logic, it deals only with *elocutio* and *pronunciatio*. Apart from this Talaeus' rhetoric is quite undistinguished.

TRAPEZUNTIUS, GEORGIUS, *Rhetoricorum libri quinque* (Venice c. 1470). This very early Renaissance rhetoric is important in renaissance tradition. From it Melancthon derived the divisions and order of treatment for his own widely disseminated texts. Books I, II and III are all concerned with *inventio*, Book IV with *dispositio* and Book V with *elocutio* and *pronunciatio*. The main authority is Hermogenes, and from Quintilian Trapezuntius takes the definition of the trope.

RHETORIC TREATISES WRITTEN IN ENGLISH

BOWES, THOMAS, *The French Academie* (1586), ed. F. J. Carpenter (Chicago, 1899). A translation of *L'Academie Française* by Pierre de la Primaudaye; a possible influence on Hoskins' *Direccions*.

COX, LEONARD, *The Arte or Crafte of Rhetoryke* (London 1530). An English translation of Book I of Melancthon's *Institutiones rhetoricae* with interpolations from Cicero's *De Inventione*. Cox deals with *inventio* and *dispositio* only.

DAY, ANGEL, *The English Secretorie or Methode of Writing of Epistles and Letters with a Declaration of such Tropes, Figures and Schemes as . . . for Ornamentsake are therein Required* (London 1592). At the end of this edition of the treatise on letter writing the tropes and schemes used are collected and briefly defined. Day also marks in the margins of his examples the various figures as they appear. He gives 16 tropes and 78 schemes. His sources of information appear to be Susenbrotus and Puttenham.

[1] For a complete bibliography of Ramist and anti-Ramist texts see W. J. Ong, *Ramus and Talon Inventory. With Agricola Checklist* (Cambridge, Mass. 1958).

FENNER, DUDLEY, *The Artes of Logike and Rethorike* (Middleburg 1584). This book is a translation of the logic of Peter Ramus and the Ramistic rhetoric of Talaeus.

FRAUNCE, ABRAHAM, *The Arcadian Rhetorike* (1588), ed. E. Seaton (London 1950). This rhetoric treatise is derived from the *Rhetorica* of Talaeus, and is concerned only with *elocutio, pronunciatio* and *memoria*. Fraunce discusses 4 tropes and 21 schemes, grouping minor figures together as examples of one more general figure. His examples are in Greek, Latin, English, French and Spanish.

HAWES, STEPHEN, *The Pastime of Pleasure* (1509), Percy Society Reprint of 1555 edition, 1845. Chapters VII-XIII of this long allegorical poem discuss *rhetoryke*. Hawes lists the divisions of rhetoric; invention, disposition, elocution, pronunciation and memory and gives some simple definitions.

HOSKINS, JOHN, *Direccions for Speech and Style* (London 1599), ed. H. Hudson (Princeton 1935). This treatise is written to a young friend of Hoskins studying law to instruct him in speech and writing. Hoskins' classification of the figures throws emphasis on what they were for. His headings include *for varying, to amplify* and *to illustrate*. The emphasis is practical.

PEACHAM, HENRY (the elder) *The Garden of Eloquence* (1st edition London 1577, a second enlarged edition London 1593), ed. W. G. Crane (Gainesville, Fla. 1954). Both editions deal with *elocutio* alone, and provide a vast number of tropes and schemes. The 1593 edition gives 19 tropes and 128 schemes. The definitions are generally standard and derivative.

PUTTENHAM, GEORGE, *The Arte of English Poesie* (London 1589), ed. A. Walker and G. D. Willcock (Cambridge 1936). This very long treatise on poetry includes a large section on the ornaments, or *elocutio*. Puttenham uses his own system to classify the devices and often gives his own original definition of the nature and function of the figure. Puttenham in the context of sixteenth-century rhetoric is very much an eccentric.

RAINOLDE, RICHARD, *A Booke Called the Foundacion of Rhetorike* (London 1563). An English translation of the *Progymnasmata* of Aphthonius from the Latin of Agricola and Cataneo.

SHERRY, RICHARD, *A Treatise of Schemes and Tropes . . . Gathered out of the Best Grammarians and Oratours* (London 1550). Sherry defines briefly 15 tropes, 67 schemes and 15 vices or faults of style. The purpose of the book is to provide a simple textbook in English for learning the methods of *elocutio*. *A Treatise of the Figures of Grammar and Rhetorike* (London 1555) is a reduced version of the former.

WILSON, THOMAS, *The Arte of Rhetorique* (London 1553). A rhetoric following the arrangement of the *Ad Herennium*. Considerable space is given to *inventio* and *dispositio*. Wilson provides his own quaint examples. Much of his material is derived directly from Cicero's *De Oratore*.

THE TEXTS USED IN COMPILING THIS WORK

APHTHONIUS SOPHISTA, *Progymnasmata Rodolpho Agricola Phrisio interprete* (Basle 1540).

AQUILA ROMANUS, *De figuris sententiarum, et elocutionis* (Venice 1523).

AUCTOR AD HERENNIUM, *Rhetorica ad Herennium*, ed. F. Marx (Leipzig 1964).

CICERO, *De Oratore*, ed. A. S. Wilkins (Oxford 1903).

 Orator, ed. A. S. Wilkins (Oxford (1903).

 Partitiones oratoriae, ed. A. S. Wilkins (Oxford 1903). The sections from the *Orator* and *De Oratore* quoted by Quintilian in Book IX of the *Institutio Oratoria*, ed. with a translation by H. E. Butler (Loeb, Cambridge, Mass. 1953).

DAY, ANGEL, *The English Secretorie or Methode of Writing of Epistles and Letters with a Declaration of Such Tropes, Figures and Schemes as either usually or for ornament-sake are therein required* (London 1625).

ERASMUS, DESIDERIUS, *On Copia of Words and Ideas*, translated by D. B. King and H. D. Rix (Milwaukee 1963).

FORTUNATIANUS, CONSULTUS CHIRIUS, *Artis rhetoricae scholicae* (Venice 1523).

FRAUNCE, ABRAHAM, *The Arcadian Rhetorike*, ed. by Ethel Seaton from the edition of 1588 (London 1950).

HOSKINS, JOHN, *Direccions for Speech and Style*, ed. by H. Hudson (Princeton 1935).

MELANCTHON, PHILIP, *De rhetorica libri tres* (Wittenburg 1519).

 Elementorum rhetorices libri duo Martin Crusii quaestionibus et scholiis explicata (Basle 1574).

 Institutiones rhetoricae (Cologne 1522).

MINTURNO, SEBASTIANI, *L'arte poetica* (Venice 1564).

PEACHAM, HENRY, *The Garden of Eloquence*, a facsimile reproduction of the 1593 and part of the 1577 editions ed. by W. G. Crane (Gainsville, Fla. 1954).

PUTTENHAM, GEORGE, *The Arte of English Poesie*, ed. by A. Walker and G. D. Willcock (Cambridge 1936).

QUINTILIAN, *Institutio Oratoria*, ed. with a translation by H. E. Butler (Loeb, Cambridge, Mass. 1953).

ROBORTELLUS, FRANCISCUS, *De artificio dicendi* (Bonn 1567).

RUFINIANUS, JULIUS, *De figuris sententiarum et elocutionis liber uno* (Basle 1521).

RUTILIUS LUPUS, PUBLIUS, *De figuris sententiarum et elocutionis* (Venice 1523).

SCALIGER, JULIUS CAESAR, *Poetices libri septem* (Heidelburg 1581).

SHERRY, RICHARD, *A Treatise of Schemes and Tropes* (London 1550).

SUSENBROTUS, JOANNES, *Epitome troporum ac schematum et grammaticorum et rhetorum* (Antwerp 1566).

TALAEUS, AUDOMARUS, *Rhetorica P. Rami praelectionibus illustrata* (Paris 1567).

TRAPEZUNTIUS, GEORGIUS, *Rhetoricorum libri quinque* (Venice 1523).

TRISSINO, GIOVANNI, *La poetica* (Vicenza 1529).

VELTKIRCHIUS, M. (John Doelsch), *Erasmus de duplicii copia verborum et rerum commentarii duo . . . ac M. Veltkirchii commentaris* (London 1569).

WILSON, THOMAS, *The Arte of Rhetorique* (1560), ed. by G. H. Mair (Oxford 1909).

The Major Systems for Dividing the Material of Traditional Rhetoric

THE DIVISIONS OF RHETORIC
IN THE RHETORICA AD HERENNIUM

The Three Kinds of Oratory	Demonstrative (occasional)	Praise or blame that may be given to a particular person or persons.
	Deliberative (political)	Counsel to persuade or dissuade the audience with respect to a particular course of action.
	Judicial (forensic)	Accusation or defence with respect to the law.
The Divisions of Rhetoric	*Inventio*	The amassing of one's material which consists of things to discuss which are true or probably true.
	Dispositio	The arrangement of one's material.
	Elocutio	The clothing of one's material in suitable words and phrases.
	Memoria	The art of remembering a speech.
	Pronunciatio	The art of delivery, by voice and gesture.
The Parts of a Speech	*Exordium* *Proemion*	The beginning whose purpose is to prepare the audience to listen with interest.
	Narratio	The exposition of pertinent topics, deeds and events.
	Divisio	When one explains what is particularly relevant to one's case and the exact nature of one's case.
	Confirmatio	The argument to support one's point of view.
	Confutatio	The dismissal of arguments against one's point of view.
	Conclusio	The artistic finish to a speech.
The Divisions of Elocutio	The Three Kinds of Style	*Gravis* (*supra*), *mediocris* and *attenuata* (*humile*).
	Exornationes verborum	Figures that affect only the words.
	Exornationes sententiarum	Figures which vary not only the words but the sense.
	10 special *exornationes verborum*	These are the tropes.

QUINTILIAN'S DIVISION OF ELOCUTIO INTO
TROPES AND SCHEMES

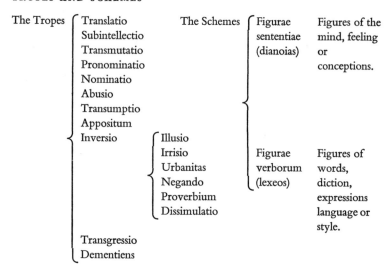

The Tropes
- Translatio
- Subintellectio
- Transmutatio
- Pronominatio
- Nominatio
- Abusio
- Transumptio
- Appositum
- Inversio
- Transgressio
- Dementiens

The Schemes
- Figurae sententiae (dianoias) — Figures of the mind, feeling or conceptions.

- Illusio
- Irrisio
- Urbanitas
- Negando
- Proverbium
- Dissimulatio

Figurae verborum (lexeos) — Figures of words, diction, expressions language or style.

TRAPEZUNTIUS' DIVISION OF RHETORIC

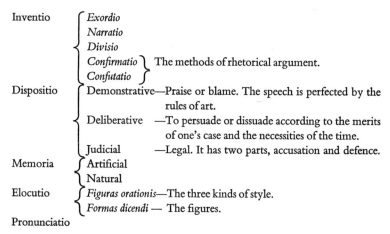

Inventio
- *Exordio*
- *Narratio*
- *Divisio*
- *Confirmatio* ⎫ The methods of rhetorical argument.
- *Confutatio* ⎭

Dispositio
- Demonstrative—Praise or blame. The speech is perfected by the rules of art.
- Deliberative —To persuade or dissuade according to the merits of one's case and the necessities of the time.
- Judicial —Legal. It has two parts, accusation and defence.

Memoria
- Artificial
- Natural

Elocutio
- *Figuras orationis*—The three kinds of style.
- *Formas dicendi* — The figures.

Pronunciatio

SCALIGER'S DIVISION OF THE FIGURES OF RHETORIC

Tropes
- Tractatio — To describe things so vividly as to place them before the eyes of the hearer or reader.
  - *Tractatio*
  - *Imago*
  - *Similitudo*
  - *Comparatio*
- Hyperbole — Excess, whether the meaning exceeds the fact or the passage is outside the basic form of the work.
  - *Dementiens*
  - *Digressio*
  - *Transitio*
- Eclipsis — When the figure works by omission.
  - *Circumlocutio*
  - *Emphasis*
  - *Invitio*
  - *Extenuatio*
  - *Aversio*
  - *Prohibitio*
- Allegoria
  - Apologue
  - Fable
  - Myth
  - Proverb
- Ironia — When the words are contrary to the sense.
  - *Irrisio*
  - *Vexatio*
  - *Negatio*
  - *Negando*
  - *Interpellatio*
  - *Admonitio*
  - *Error*

Figures
- By their nature
  - omission
  - addition
- According to their position
  - Disorder
  - Parenthesis
  - Division and rearrangement
  - *Adjunctio* (zeugma)
- By reason of number or quantity
- By reason of sound
  - *Similiter cadens*
  - Rhyme

THE RAMISTIC DIVISION OF RHETORIC BY FRAUNCE

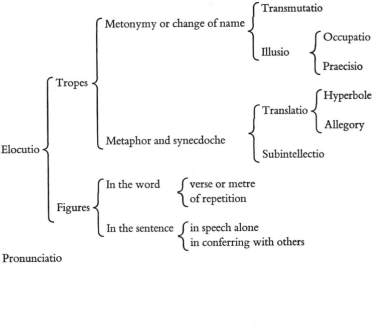

Pronunciatio

Descriptive Index of Tropes and Schemes

The purpose of this index is to assist the reader to identify a trope or scheme if he has a description of it but does not have its name. The name given in the index is the one under which the figure appears in this book. The figure may also have other names which are given with its description.

FIGURES OF ADDITION—DIGRESSIONS ETC.

Acervatio	The use of as many different conjunctions as possible.[1]	19
Adinventio	The addition of a prepared excuse to confront all possible objections.	20
Adjudicatio	An opinion or judgment added to a saying from some other author.	20
Aenos	The moral added to a fable.	191
Attemperatio	The addition of statements, general truths, etc. to confirm the truth of a proposition.	33
Circumductio	When superfluous words are inserted into a speech.	37

[1] These descriptions are aids to finding the figures in this book and not historically accurate definitions.

FIGURES OF ADMISSION AND CONCESSION

FIGURES WHICH AMPLIFY THE IMPORTANCE OF THE SUBJECT OF DISCOURSE

FIGURES OF APPEAL TO THE AUDIENCE (by threat or promise or entreaty)

FIGURES FOR ENDING

FIGURES WHICH EXAGGERATE OR DIMINISH

TROPES (All tropes involve words used to mean something other than their normal meaning)

Index of Greek Terms

Index of Latin Terms[1]

[1] Some of these terms are of Greek origin and regularly used in Latinate form.

Index of Italian Terms